Mario Kos

Sicily

Arnone Editore - Palermo

© Copyright 2001 by ARNONE Editore s.r.l.
Offices and Administration: Via Francesco Crispi 120 - 90139 Palermo (Italy) - Tel./Fax 0916 124 007
Depot: Via Filippo Patti 25 - 90133 Palermo - Tel. 091 333 461 - Fax 091 333 484
http://www.arnoneeditore.com • Email: info@arnoneeditore.com

Text: Mario Kos

Photographs: Lanfranco Angeli, Franco Amico, Paolo Arnone, Enzo Lo Verso,
Foto Patti, Publifoto, Saverio Rao, Carmelo Sammarco, Arnone Editore Archives

All photographs property of ARNONE Editore s.r.l.

Layout, graphics, cover and image research: Saverio Rao
Translation: Quid Traduzioni e Servizi Linguistici – Palermo (Claudia Ricchiari)
Image digitization: Litoscanner - Palermo
Printed and bound by: Officine Grafiche Riunite - Palermo

ISBN 88-87663-38-6

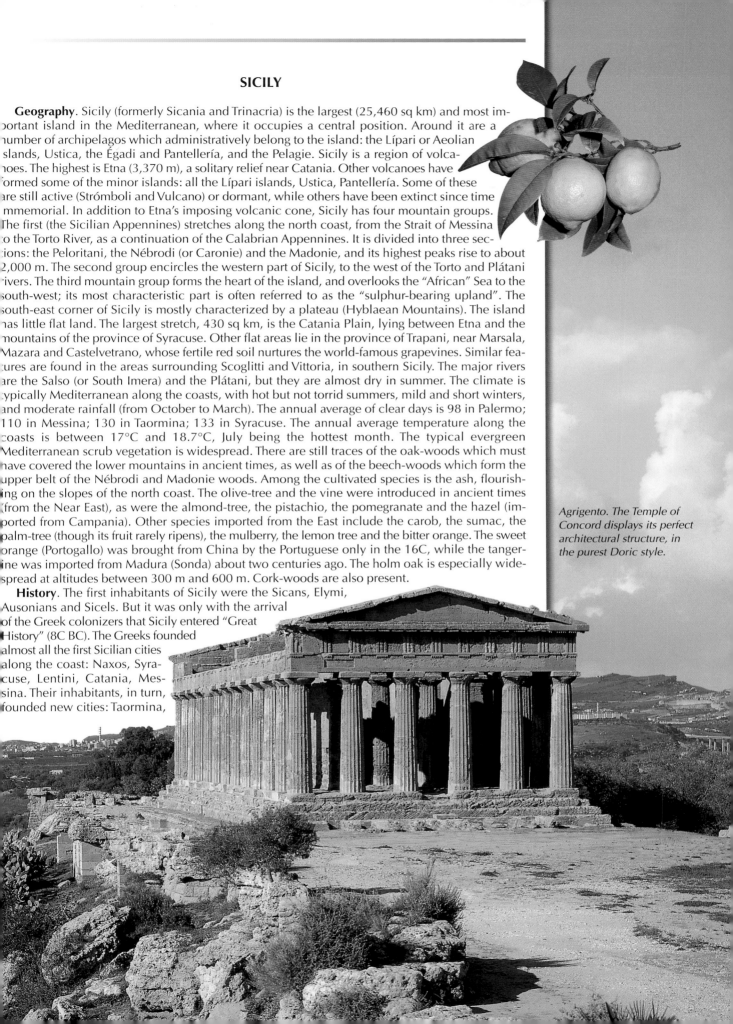

SICILY

Geography. Sicily (formerly Sicania and Trinacria) is the largest (25,460 sq km) and most important island in the Mediterranean, where it occupies a central position. Around it are a number of archipelagos which administratively belong to the island: the Lípari or Aeolian islands, Ustica, the Égadi and Pantellería, and the Pelagie. Sicily is a region of volcanoes. The highest is Etna (3,370 m), a solitary relief near Catania. Other volcanoes have formed some of the minor islands: all the Lípari islands, Ustica, Pantellería. Some of these are still active (Strómboli and Vulcano) or dormant, while others have been extinct since time immemorial. In addition to Etna's imposing volcanic cone, Sicily has four mountain groups. The first (the Sicilian Appennines) stretches along the north coast, from the Strait of Messina to the Torto River, as a continuation of the Calabrian Appennines. It is divided into three sections: the Peloritani, the Nébrodi (or Caronie) and the Madonie, and its highest peaks rise to about 2,000 m. The second group encircles the western part of Sicily, to the west of the Torto and Plátani rivers. The third mountain group forms the heart of the island, and overlooks the "African" Sea to the south-west; its most characteristic part is often referred to as the "sulphur-bearing upland". The south-east corner of Sicily is mostly characterized by a plateau (Hyblaean Mountains). The island has little flat land. The largest stretch, 430 sq km, is the Catania Plain, lying between Etna and the mountains of the province of Syracuse. Other flat areas lie in the province of Trapani, near Marsala, Mazara and Castelvetrano, whose fertile red soil nurtures the world-famous grapevines. Similar features are found in the areas surrounding Scoglitti and Vittoria, in southern Sicily. The major rivers are the Salso (or South Imera) and the Plátani, but they are almost dry in summer. The climate is typically Mediterranean along the coasts, with hot but not torrid summers, mild and short winters, and moderate rainfall (from October to March). The annual average of clear days is 98 in Palermo; 110 in Messina; 130 in Taormina; 133 in Syracuse. The annual average temperature along the coasts is between 17°C and 18.7°C, July being the hottest month. The typical evergreen Mediterranean scrub vegetation is widespread. There are still traces of the oak-woods which must have covered the lower mountains in ancient times, as well as of the beech-woods which form the upper belt of the Nébrodi and Madonie woods. Among the cultivated species is the ash, flourishing on the slopes of the north coast. The olive-tree and the vine were introduced in ancient times (from the Near East), as were the almond-tree, the pistachio, the pomegranate and the hazel (imported from Campania). Other species imported from the East include the carob, the sumac, the palm-tree (though its fruit rarely ripens), the mulberry, the lemon tree and the bitter orange. The sweet orange (Portogallo) was brought from China by the Portuguese only in the 16C, while the tangerine was imported from Madura (Sonda) about two centuries ago. The holm oak is especially widespread at altitudes between 300 m and 600 m. Cork-woods are also present.

History. The first inhabitants of Sicily were the Sicans, Elymi, Ausonians and Sicels. But it was only with the arrival of the Greek colonizers that Sicily entered "Great History" (8C BC). The Greeks founded almost all the first Sicilian cities along the coast: Naxos, Syracuse, Lentini, Catania, Messina. Their inhabitants, in turn, founded new cities: Taormina,

Agrigento. The Temple of Concord displays its perfect architectural structure, in the purest Doric style.

Palermo. Archaeological Museum. Lèkythos depicting a "Departing warrior", by a painter from Haimon, 500-475 BC.

Bottom: Taormina. A suggestive view of the Greek theatre, 3C BC.

Megara Hyblaea, Gela, Selinunte, Himera, Milazzo, Agrigento, Segesta, Lilybaeum, etc. These cities were first ruled by Oligarchies and later by Tyrannies. The most powerful Tyranny was that of Syracuse, which eventually subjugated all the other cities. But it soon came into conflict with Carthage, which had managed to consolidate its presence in the western tip of Sicily, taking control of Motya, Panormos and Solunto. The conflict ended with the victory of the Syracusans in the battle fought at Himera (480 BC). The war between the two powers, however, continued with alternating fortunes until Rome took the place of Syracuse, inheriting its historical role. Only after the three Punic Wars and the destruction of the Carthaginian Empire did the Romans gain effective control of Sicily. The island was then made into a Province, with a Praetor in Syracuse and two Quaestors, one in Syracuse and the other at Lilybaeum. Sicilian agriculture was strongly developed under Roman rule, and the island enjoyed a period of peace which lasted for centuries. It later passed under the jurisdiction of the Eastern Roman Empire, and a new era of peace began, with the introduction of the Christian faith and of Byzantine culture. In 827, however, the island was invaded by the Saracens, who imposed their iron rule. During the second half of the 11C, a Christian army led by Robert "the Guiscard" and his brother Roger I of Hauteville, who had been mandated by the Pope in Rome, freed the island from Arab control. In 1130 the Kingdom of Sicily was created and, at Christmas that same year, Roger II of Hauteville was proclaimed first king of Sicily. He extended the Sicilian dominion, creating a vast kingdom which stretched from Montecassino to Albania and the North African coasts of Tunisia and Libya. The Hauteville dynasty gave another two great sovereigns to Sicily, William I and his son William II. Men of science and letters, politicians and artists from all over the world gathered at Palermo's court, turning it into a magnificent centre of international culture. After the death of William II, in 1189, the Hauteville dynasty was replaced by that of the Hohenstaufens. The short and tragic reign of Henry VI was followed by a return to ancient splendour in 1208, with the accession to the throne of Henry's son, the great Frederick (I of Sicily; II of the Empire). A great statesman, well-versed in administration, natural science and mathematics, he promoted the development of a new, pre-Renaissance culture at his court. On his death (1250), a period of political unrest began. The crown of Sicily (a vassal of the Holy See) was assigned by the Pope to Charles of Anjou, the brother of the king of France. The Angevins (French) went so far as to subject Sicily to military occupation. This led to the Vespers Revolution, which broke out in Palermo on Easter Monday 1282, causing the expulsion of the Angevins from the island. The legitimate heir to the throne was King Peter of Aragon who, supported by the Sicilian nobility, was crowned King of Sicily in Palermo on 4 September 1282. With the only exception of Frederick II of Sicily, the Aragonese dynasty of Sicily (Crown of Trinacria), which had replaced the Angevins (supported by France), proved to be weak. In the 14C, in fact, the great aristocratic families gained effective control of the island thanks to their economic and military power. The most important – the Alagona, Peralta, Ventimiglia and Chiaramonte families – as a matter of fact divided Sicily into four spheres of influence. This was the period of the four Vicars. In 1392 – after about one century of political weakness on the part of the Crown of Trinacria, and after the doubtful outcome of the Vespers War against the Angevins of Naples (they maintained the title of kings of Sicily) – the Aragonese of Spain strongly repressed Sicilian aspirations to autonomy. In 1415, Sicily was joined to the Crown of Aragon and was thus ruled by viceroys. In the 15C King Alfonso "the Magnanimous" (of Aragon and Sicily) managed to reunite the two parts of the ancient State (Sicily and southern Italy), which he refounded as the Kingdom of the two Sicilies. France fomented a series of revolts, which broke out between the 16C and the 17C. In 1672, during the war against Spain, Messina eventually rose up in arms, openly supported by the France of Louis XIV. But, in spite of their victories at sea and on land, in 1678 the French abandoned Augusta and Messina; the latter was severely punished by the Crown, and thus entered an irresistible process of decline. At the beginning of the 18C, Sicily was involved in the Spanish and Polish wars of succession (1700-1738). During

a thirty-year period, the island was forced to yield its crown first to the Savoy dynasty, then to the emperor of Austria Charles VI and, finally, to the Spanish Charles of Bourbon, who began the dynasty of the Bourbons of Naples and restored the autonomy of the Kingdom of Naples and Sicily. Due to the French invasion, King Ferdinand of Bourbon moved to Palermo for a few years. Here he had to yield to the aspirations to autonomy of the aristocracy by promulgating a Constitution (1812). However, when monarchic authority was restored in 1816, he repudiated the Constitution and dissolved the Sicilian Parliament. In 1820-21 the first anti-Bourbon uprising broke out. During the Revolution of 1848, the supporters of the cause of independence created an autonomous Parliament in Naples, and later proposed that an independent Sicily and the other Italian States should join to form a federation. The Revolution was put down by military force. The war of 1860-61 eventually ended with the annexation of Sicily and southern Italy to the Kingdom of Italy, ruled by the House of Savoy. On 15 May 1946, a legislative decree granted regional autonomy to Sicily on the basis of a special Statute. In April 1947, the first Sicilian Regional Parliament was appointed.

King Roger II crowned by Christ. Mosaic dating from the first half of the 12C, in the Church of the Martorana, Palermo. The iconographic model is that of the coronation ceremonies of the Byzantine emperors in Constantinople of the same period.

Art. The imposing architectural remains of temples, theatres and aqueducts which still rise majestically on the sites of great ancient cities, as well as the large number of fine sculptures, decorative features of ancient buildings, pottery and precious items displayed in the main archaeological museums in Sicily, all bear witness to centuries of Graeco-Sicel, Roman and Byzantine culture, making up one of the most remarkable archaeological treasures of all mankind. The temples of Segesta, Selinunte and Agrigento, the theatres of Taormina, Syracuse and Selinunte, the aqueducts of Termini and Agrigento, the defensive works of Syracuse (the Euryalus Castle), the archaeological museums in Syracuse, Palermo, Trapani, Himera, etc., as well as the vast archaeological sites of ancient cities such as Agrigento, Heraclea Minoa, Himera, Segesta, Selinunte, etc., cannot be easily summarized here. For brevity's sake, we can say that Sicilian art of antiquity was characterized by the presence of majestic architectural works in cities which astonished the Ancient World with their dimensions. Characteristic features of this art were the highly-developed technical skills (particularly in the field of water-conveying systems), the magnificence of the Roman patrician villas, the refined statuary and the richness and realism of the great mosaic cycles. All these features flourished again both under the Byzantines and in the Middle Ages, when the rest of western Europe was still struggling to free itself from a semi-barbarian condition. Sicilian medieval art in the first decades of the Kingdom (from the end of the 11C through the 12C) was characterized by the fact that almost all the works were commissioned and financed by the Crown. Thanks to their prerogatives as "papal legates", the members of the Hauteville dynasty were able to build the first

great Latin cathedrals (Messina; Lipari; Cefalù; Monreale; Catania; Mazara; Agrigento; etc.). In these churches, the new Latin architectural spatiality imported from central Italy and northern Europe combined with the sumptuous decoration from the Maghreb, with the narrative schemes of Byzantine mosaics, and with Apulian Romanesque sculpture. Roger II built Cefalù Cathedral, where he wished to be buried. Later, he had his Royal Palace erected in Palermo, with his own Palace Chapel (the "Palatine Chapel"), the most magnificent example of Sicilian medieval art, built in 1132 and dedicated to St Peter. The Royal Palace also housed the royal art and crafts workshops, where crowns, jewels, precious furnishings and ceremonial clothes were made. Some of these can still be admired today, such as the splendid Byzantine imperial crown (*Kamelaukion*) now displayed in the Cathedral Treasury. Roger II was succeeded by William I, who built the Zisa royal residence within the great royal park. His son, William II, built the Cuba and the majestic Duomo of Monreale, another jewel of royal art. The interior is richly decorated with splendid Byzantine mosaics, and the cloister is one of the most elegant expressions of medieval sculpture applied to architecture. In the meantime, the old Palermo Cathedral was partially demolished and reconstructed as a much larger building on the initiative of Bishop Gualtiero, who transformed it into the greatest cathedral of medieval Sicily. The age of Emperor Frederick II Hohenstaufen was mainly characterized by the building of his castles, which represent a "*unicum*" in world history. The residential needs of the sovereign and defensive needs were combined and satisfied in constructions of refined formal elegance: the Ursino Castle (Catania); the Maniace Castle (Syracuse) and the Castles of Augusta and Milazzo, as well as the Towers of Enna, of the Colombaia in Trapani, and of Gela. In the 14C, due to the Vespers War and to Baronial Anarchy, Sicily withdrew into itself, and the art it produced was a mere continuation of the expressive forms which had characterized the previous age. In the 15C, however, the first step was taken towards a new aesthetic taste. The most outstanding figure in architecture was Matteo Carnelivari of Noto, who was active in Palermo towards the end of the century (Palazzo Abatellis, Palazzo Aiutamicristo and the Church of Santa Maria della Catena). Antonello da Messina (1430-1479) is the greatest Sicilian painter of all time, and one of the greatest 15C masters in Europe. Some of his paintings have remained in Sicily: *the Portrait of an Unknown Seaman*, in the Cefalù Mandralisca Museum, the *Three Saints* and the splendid *Annunziata* in the Palermo Gallery, the San Gregorio polyptych in the Messina Museum, and the *Annunciation* in the Palazzo Bellomo Museum in Syracuse. In sculpture, the most outstanding figure was Domenico Gagini (Bissone c 1420 – Palermo 1492), the founder of a workshop which, for many generations, held a prominent position in the field. In the 16C, the expressive forms of Tuscan and Roman Mannerism began to gain ground. The leading figures were: Antonello Gagini (1478-1536) and Polidoro da Caravaggio (the author of two fine lateral doors in the Duomo of Messina). When Antonello died, his work was continued by his sons. Many Tuscan sculptors moved to

Sicily during the 16C, including Montorsoli (famous for the fountains of Orion and Neptune; the *Scylla*, now in the Messina Museum). Among his disciples were Martino Montanini and A. Calamech. In architecture, the forms of Mannerism became popular in the first half of the 17C. Examples of this are, in Palermo: the Quattro Canti (Giulio Lasso); Porta Felice (Pietro Novelli); the churches of Olivella and San Domenico; the old Shipyard (Mariano Smiriglio); the Church of the Teatini (Giacomo Besio). And also: the Town Hall in Syracuse (G. Vermexio); the Benedectine Monastery in Catania (V. De Franchis); the College and Church of the Jesuits in Trapani (N. Masuccio). Baroque art was inaugurated by the church of the Annunziata dei Teatini in Messina (Guarino Guarini). It took more austere forms in Palermo with Paolo Amato (1634-1714): Church of the Salvatore; and Giacomo Amato (1643-1732): Church of the Pietà and Santa Teresa alla Kalsa. The famous Villas of Bagheria are a case apart: here the architects' creativity is reflected in the scenographic architectural design and sinuous external staircases (Villa Palagonia; Villa Valguarnera; etc., 18C). More fanciful baroque forms characterize the towns rebuilt after the 1693 earthquake (Catania, Syracuse, Noto, Grammichele, Avola, Ragusa, Modica, etc.). The Palermitan Vaccarini planned the reconstruction work in Catania (façade of the Cathedral; Palazzo Valle; the Town Hall; St Agatha's Abbey). Rosario Gagliardi (1726-1770) was active in different centres: Noto, Ragusa, Comiso, Caltagirone. His works include the churches of San Domenico and of the Collegio (Noto), those of San Giorgio and San Giuseppe (Ragusa) and the Cathedral of Modica. All these works are characterized by plastic structures and dynamic and original outlines. In painting, the most outstanding figure was P. Novelli of Monreale (1603-1647). His works include the paintings in the Capuchin churches at Ragusa and Leonforte, a large painting in Monreale, and a *St Christopher* in the Catania Museum. Vito D'Anna (1720-1769) can be considered the founder of the school of Sicilian fresco painters of the second half of the century. In sculpture, Giacomo Serpotta (1656-1732) occupies a place of his own. The descendant of a family of sculptors and plastic artists, he was active in Palermo, where he decorated with joyful stuccoes a large number of churches and oratories (Oratories of San Lorenzo, Santa Cita, etc.). Another great sculptor and plastic artist was Ignazio Marabitti (1719-1797) (marble altarpiece of the *Apotheosis of St Benedict* in the Duomo of Monreale). 19C architecture began with the neoclassical work of the Palermitan G. V. Marvuglia (1729-1814), including the Oratory of San Filippo Neri all'Olivella and Villa Belmonte, in the Acquasanta quarter (Palermo). The most outstanding figures of late-19C architecture were the Palermitans G. B. F. Basile (Teatro Massimo) and G. Damiani Almeyda (Politeama Garibaldi). The period between the 19C and the 20C was dominated by the architect Ernesto Basile, a talented designer who introduced a refined and independent Sicilian Liberty style, a forerunner of Rationalism. Among his disciples were several distinguished architects.

Traditions. Sicily still retains some of its age-old traditions both in the working and social fields. Tunny fishing, for example, still uses the traditional techniques ("tonnare"), as does swordfish fishing in the Strait of Messina. The production of ceramic articles is still considerable. Excellent Sicilian wines are still appreciated worldwide. Among local religious cults, the celebrations in honour of the patron saints are of particular interest. The most famous of these is the so-called *Festino* of St Rosalia in Palermo (13-15 July), characterized by the Processions of the Triumphal Chariot and of the silver urn of the *Santuzza*, as Palermitans call their patron saint. Messina celebrates the feast of the Mid-August Madonna (15 August) with the procession of the *vara* (processional bier) of Our Lady of the Assumption and of the two Giants on horseback, the mythical forefathers of the people of Messina. Catania celebrates St Agatha, the patron saint, by carrying her reliquary laden with precious objects through the city streets, pulled by dozens of believers wearing the traditional white "sackcloth" (in February). But the scenographic forms taken by these festivals are innumerable, and each town and village in Sicily has its own. Besides local saints' festivals, the religious celebrations of the Holy Week are also of deep significance for Sicilian people. Particularly suggestive are those held in Enna, Caltanissetta and Trapani. A cycle of celebrations with different characteristics is that of the Byzantine Holy Week at Piana degli Albanesi.

Palermo. Mount Pellegrino. Engravings in the "Addaura 2" cave, detail.

Below: A suggestive view of Palermo from Mount Pellegrino.

PALERMO

The name Palermo derives from the Greek word *Panormos*, meaning "all port". In fact, it was the spacious natural harbour that favoured the earliest settlements and the founding of the city on an oblong rocky spur bounded to the north by the Papireto River and to the south by the Kemonia. The ancient port, of which only the present-day Cala remains, lays between the mouths of the two rivers. Evidence exists of the presence of different peoples in the area: the Sicans in the 12C BC, followed by the Cypriots, Cretans, Elymi and Greeks. The first permanent urban settlement, however, was founded by the Phoenicians between the 8C and the 7C BC. The *Paleapolis* (from the Greek "old city") lays on the upper part of the oblong rocky spur and was surrounded by strong city walls. A second city, the *Neapolis* (from the Greek "new city"), was later built between the two rivers, but outside the city walls and closer to the port. Between 485 BC and 306 BC Panormos was involved in the long-lasting struggle for supremacy between the Greeks and Carthaginians. From 254 BC, the city was ruled by the Romans. Christianity soon flourished and spread, as is witnessed by the presence of a series of catacombs, including the famous ones of the Papireto (Porta d'Ossuna). In 536, the Gothic garrison which had occupied the city was driven out by the Byzantine general Belisarius, and Palermo passed under the rule of Constantinople, which had reunited the Roman Empire. The first Cathedral was built between 590 and 604 on the initiative of Bishop Victor. Two Palermitans, Agatho and Sergius, became Roman Popes and were later canonized. The city was stormed by the Saracens in 831, after a one-year heroic resistance.

In 1072, Palermo was liberated by a Christian army led by the Hauteville brothers, Roger (Great Count of Sicily) and Robert ("the Guiscard"), and regained its ancient splendour. In 1130, in fact, it became the capital of the Kingdom of Sicily and on Christmas Day that same year the first king, Roger II of Hauteville, was crowned in the Cathedral, which was restored to the Christian cult. Trade and cultural activities had already recovered and were flourishing again, favoured by Palermo's position as the capital of a great cosmopolitan kingdom. Roger II added architectural splendour to the *Castrum Superius*, which became his Royal Palace. Inside this complex construction, in 1132, he built his Palace chapel (the "Palatine Chapel"), dedicated to St Peter, which is the most magnificent example of medieval art in Palermo. Meanwhile, the city was enriched with splendid buildings: the

churches of San Giovanni dei Lebbrosi, San Giovanni degli Eremiti, San Cataldo, Santa Maria dell'Ammiraglio (the "Martorana"). Just outside the city walls, Roger II created a large park with woods, plantations, stock farms, artificial lakes and luxury royal residences: Maredolce, Favara, Parco (Altofonte). Roger II was suceeded by William I, who built the Zisa royal residence within the great Royal Park. His successor, William II, built the Cuba. During his reign the Hauteville dynasty reached the height of international prestige. He promoted the construction, within the boundaries of the Royal Park, of the great Duomo of Monreale and of the nearby Benedictine monastery and Royal Palace. The church is another gem of medieval architecture in Sicily. The interior is richly decorated with splendid Byzantine mosaics and the cloister is one of the highest expressions of Romanesque sculpture applied to architecture. In the meantime, from 1170 to 1184, the old Palermo Cathedral was partially demolished and reconstructed as a much larger building on the initiative of Bishop Gualtiero, who transformed it into the greatest cathedral of medieval Sicily. In the 12C, Palermo was the splendid capital of the first Italian unitary State after the collapse of the Western Roman Empire.

The Hauteville dynasty was followed by that of the Hohenstaufens, with Emperors Henry VI and Frederick II. The reign of Frederick II was of no advantage to Palermo. On his death (1250), a period of political unrest began, which certainly did not benefit the city. Palermo thus started to slowly lose its role of predominance, while Naples was gradually increasing its prestige. The crown of Sicily (a vassal of the Holy See) was assigned by the Pope to Charles of Anjou, the brother of the king of France. The Angevins (French) went so far as to subject Sicily to military occupation. This led to the "Vespers Revolution", which broke out in Palermo on Easter Monday 1282, causing the expulsion of the Angevins from the island. The legitimate heir to the throne was King Peter of Aragon who, supported by the Sicilian nobility, was crowned king of Sicily in Palermo on 4 September 1282. This marked the beginning of the weak dynasty of the Aragonese of Sicily, who became subject to the great aristocratic families. In the 14C Palermo was in fact under the rule of the powerful Chiaramonte family. But, in 1392, the Aragonese of Spain put an end to these aspirations to autonomy. Andrea Chiaramonte, the only one of the four Vicars who resisted the troops of Martin of Aragon, was captured and beheaded in the Piano della Marina, the square overlooked by his sumptuous Palermitan palace, the *Steri*, which can still be admired today. In 1415 the crown of Sicily was joined to the

Palermo. The Kamelaukion (calotte crown) of the Sicilian sovereigns, in the Cathedral Treasury.

crown of Aragon, and the island was ruled by viceroys. These alternately resided in the Chiaramonte family's *Steri* or in the Castellammare (the sea castle), and only at a later time, in the 16C, in the ancient Royal Palace. 15C art was characterized by the "Sicilian Gothic" style, bearing Catalan influences. The most outstanding architect of the time was Matteo Carnelivari of Noto, to whom the elegant Church of Santa Maria della Catena, in the Cala quarter, has been attributed. Carnelivari also designed Palazzo Abatellis and Palazzo Aiutamicristo (1490), chosen by Charles V and Don John of Austria as their residences in the following century. Between the 15C and the 16C, new impulse was given to Palermitan sculpture by the workshop of the Gagini, a family of skilful sculptors and stucco decorators (Domenico, Antonello and a host of relatives). The Gagini did not confine their work to sculpturing single statues of Madonnas and Saints, but inserted them into magnificent architectural ensembles, enriched with frames, panels, balustrades depicting stories of the Saints and delicate decorative motifs, which embellished church apses and chapels, thus introducing Tuscan Renaissance taste into Palermo.

In the 17C-18C, architectural activity was promoted not only by the city Senate, but also by two important groups of clients: the Aristocracy and the religious Orders. The great aristocratic families built sumptuous palaces which were unequalled in Europe. Palazzo Villafranca, Palazzo Ugo, Palazzo Belmonte and Palazzo Riso were erected in Piazza Bologni, Palermo's aristocratic showcase. The majestic Palazzo Trabia rose along the Marina promenade. An entire new street, the *Strada Nova* (the present-day Via Maqueda) was started in 1600 to allow the building of new aristocratic palaces (the most important being Palazzo Comitini). At the crossroads of the *Strada Nova* and the *Cassaro* was, and still is, Piazza Vigliena (also known as the Octagon, the Theatre of the Sun, or the Four Corners of the City), the heart of 17C-18C Palermo. The religious Orders entrusted their "architects in cassocks" (who had been the disciples of the masters of Mannerism and Baroque, in Rome) with the design of religious houses, churches, monasteries and convents. All these buildings contributed to Palermo's architectural grandeur: from the Jesuit Casa Professa to San Giuseppe dei Teatini; from Santa Teresa alla Kalsa to San Domenico; from San Francesco Saverio to Sant'Anna. The prevailing style in architecture was, at this time, Mannerism. Baroque taste was only limited to the internal decoration of most of the churches and of some of the palaces. Church interiors, in particular, were sumptuously decorated with polychrome marble inlays, stuccoed human figures and ornamental motifs, skilfully executed ironwork, polychrome floors, not to mention paintings and furnishings. In sculpture, Palermo outclassed the rest of Italy with the greatest stucco decorator of all time: Giacomo Serpotta (1656-1732), the author of the splendid stuccoes in the Oratories of Santa Cita, the Rosario and San Lorenzo. His work was continued by his son Procopio and by numerous disciples. Great names in painting were those of Pietro Novelli (1603-1647), Filippo Paladini, Vito d'Anna and Antonio Grano. At this time, public festivals – both lay and religious – were at the height of their splendour, also thanks to the rich scenographic ensembles, to the external decorations of churches and palaces, to the magnificent Triumphal Chariots of St Rosalia (the city's patron saint) and to the "firework display machines".

Between the 18C and the 19C, the architect Venanzio Marvuglia designed the Riso, Geraci, Costantino and Coglitore Palaces, the Oratory of San Filippo Neri, Villa Belmonte and the Palazzina Cinese. In the 19C, the architect G. B. Filippo Basile designed the greatest opera house in Italy, the Teatro Massimo, which was commenced in 1875 and completed in 1897, while the engineer Giuseppe Damiani Almeyda designed the Politeama Garibaldi, erected in 1874. Later, thanks to the elegant work of Ernesto Basile, Filippo's son, Palermo became the Italian capital of the *liberty* architectural style. Among his best-known works are: the Villa Igiea Hotel, Villa Florio, the Florio Pavilion, Villa Deliella (no longer extant), Villa Basile, the Kursaal Biondo, the seat of the Cassa di Risparmio, etc. The best painter of the time was Francesco Lojacono; in sculpture, the best-known artist was Mario Rutelli. Meanwhile, Palermo was expanding beyond its ancient walls, onto the area previously used for the great National Exhibition of 1891. The "middle-class" part of the city was thus created. In the 1950s, crowds of people from the neighbouring provinces arrived in Palermo, mostly attracted by the prospects of a job in the regional administration, resulting in an enormous building expansion.

ROYAL PALACE: THE SEAT OF THE SICILIAN SOVEREIGNS AND THE PALATINE CHAPEL

From the earliest centuries of its history, Palermo had a fortified government building on the site now occupied by the Royal Palace. This was used and enlarged by the Romans, Byzantines and Saracens. Around 1130 Roger II of Hauteville, the first king of Sicily, had the remains of this ancient construction covered with earth so that a hill was formed, on which he built his own Royal Palace. The magnificent building was intended to embody all the prerogatives of a royal palace and, at the same time, to be one of the main strongholds in the city. In fact, it was called *Castrum Superius* to distinguish it from the Castellammare near the port, or *Castrum Inferius*. It housed the Royal apartments, covered with marble and mosaics, the Throne Room, the Palace Chapel and the Treasury Room. But there were also government offices, stables and kitchens, barracks and prisons, as well as the renowned *Officinae* where

Palermo. Royal Palace. East front looking onto the old town.

Greek, Berber and Jewish workwomen (the famous maids from whom medieval sovereigns in Palermo chose their mistresses) made the Crown jewels, the king's ceremonial clothes, furnishings for the daily life of the royal family, etc. The Palatine Chapel (1143) – dedicated to St Peter, the patron saint of the Latin Church – can be compared to an exquisite casket full of precious works of art. It harmoniously combines the cultural and aesthetic influences of the peoples who were then ruled by the king of Sicily – Latins, Graeco-Byzantines, Lombards, Berbers and Arabs – as well as artists from far-away Persia. A jewel in its own right, it is one of the masterpieces of medieval religious art. From the second half of the 13C, the great architectural complex of the Royal Palace was abandoned by the sovereigns and began to fall into decay. Restoration work began around the mid-16C under Emperor Charles V. A great external bastion (still extant) was built, while the higher parts of the towers (which had become easy targets for siege batteries) were demolished. In the 17C and 18C the viceroys ordered further restoration and new works. The two great internal courtyards (the Maqueda and Fountain Courtyards) were laid out with porticoes and loggias, and the monumental east façade was built. The new halls housed the meetings of the Sicilian Parliament and became the residence of the viceroys. During the struggles for autonomy in 1848 the Royal Palace was assailed and sacked by the rebels, who took away several works of art and demolished two bulwarks which had been built in the 17C on the main façade. Repairs and refurbishment were carried out by the Bourbon restoration but new damage was caused by the American army of occupation in 1943-44. In the post-war period the building became the seat of the Sicilian Regional Assembly under the curious name of "The Norman Palace". The medieval structures still existing today are King Roger's Rooms, the Palatine Chapel, the Pisana Tower and the underground rooms. Recently, during deep archaeological excavations in the basement of a wing of the Palace, a long stretch of the Punic-Roman city walls was brought to light, including a city gate. The walls are made of large square-cut and skilfully arranged stones (Hellenic technique) and probably date from the end of the 5C BC. With their imposing structure, they are an extremely suggestive sight.

Palermo. Royal Palace, King Roger's Rooms. Facing peacocks (12C mosaic).

"KING ROGER'S ROOMS"

The most obvious remains of the royal apartments ("Joaria") can be found in the Room of the Winds (formerly roofless) and the so-called King Roger's Room, still covered with the original mosaics depicting hunting scenes (perhaps referring to the nearby Royal Park), animals and plants, including several exotic species. The style is that of the well-known mosaic cycles of the Great Hunts which decorated

the majestic villas of both late-Roman Sicily and Roman-Byzantine North Africa. No other European sovereign of the 12C could boast apartments as grandly decorated as those of the king in Palermo.

THE PALATINE CHAPEL

The construction of this chapel began in 1130, immediately after the coronation of Roger II as the first sovereign of the Kingdom of Sicily. It was consecrated on 28 April 1140 and dedicated to St Peter in honour of the Pope in Rome, the feudal Lord of the Sicilian State. The building was designed as a combination of the "Latin" nave and aisles with a Byzantine raised sanctuary, covered by a dome and with three apses facing east. This was the "mixed" plan which was to become a model for several Sicilian churches in the Middle

Opposite page, top: Palermo.
Royal Palace, King Roger's
Room.

Opposite page, bottom:
Royal Palace, Palatine Chapel.
Central apse.

Royal Palace, Palatine Chapel.
Mosaics depicting the Nativity
and the Entry of Christ into
Jerusalem.

Palermo. Royal Palace, Palatine Chapel. Christ Pantocrator in the bowl-shaped vault of the central apse.

Ages. It extends over 32 m in length, with the nave and two aisles divided by two rows of five columns each (in Egyptian and cipolin marble). The Chapel is 12.50 m wide and 12.40 m high (18 m in the dome). The interior is like a precious casket full of art treasures which, in spite of their different cultural origins, are combined in a harmonious aesthetic whole. Both the wall mosaics and the geometric mosaics covering the floor are Byzantine, with Christ Pantocrator depicted both in the cupola and in the bowl-shaped vault of the central apse. The magnificent wooden lacunar with its complex star-like design is the work of craftsmen from the Maghreb, while the decorations in the honeycomb-like carvings were carried out by westernized Persian painters. Sculptural works, both free-standing (pulpit, Paschal candlestick, etc.) and decorative (capitals, frames, bases, etc.) belong to the aesthetic tradition of the Latin Romanesque style.

PORTA NUOVA

The earliest architectural forms of this gate date back to 1420. Built to celebrate the entry into Palermo of King Alfonso "the Magnanimous" (of Sicily and Aragon), the original gate corresponded to the lower part of the present-day one and was in the style of a Roman triumphal arch. Later, in 1583-84, the gate was restructured to celebrate the triumphal entry into Palermo of Emperor Charles V after his conquest of Tunis (1535), with the addition of the majestic upper loggia and pyramidal cusp with a small lantern on the top. The majolica tile covering on the two main fronts of the pyramid depicts the imperial eagle. Two imposing pairs of statues, representing captive Moors, were also added to the west side of the gate.

CHURCH OF SAN GIOVANNI DEGLI EREMITI

In the 6C AD the site of the present-day building was occupied by a monastery ordered by Pope Gregory the Great and dedicated to St Hermes. Later on, during Arab rule, the architectural complex underwent some alterations and was used as a mosque. Between 1142 and 1148 it was further transformed and restored to the Christian cult; both church and monastery were then assigned to monks from Campania. Apparently, all the princes of the Hauteville dynasty who were not to succeed to the throne were buried in this monastery in the 12C, but no traces of their tombs have remained. The present aspect of the building, one of the most fascinating medieval monuments in Palermo, clearly reflects its complex architectural history. The church is covered by six cupolas – two larger ones on the single nave, three smaller ones on the transept and one on the bell tower. The cloister is particularly suggestive, with its small twin columns supporting pointed arches invigorated by the double projection of the frames. Together with the architectural features of the complex, the luxuriant vegetation contributes to create a unique romantic atmosphere.

Above: West side of the Porta Nuova.

Below: Palermo. Church of San Giovanni degli Eremiti, the Cloister.

THE CATHEDRAL

This majestic building, as it can be seen today, is the outcome of a long series of alterations, demolitions and additions carried out in various periods, from before the year 1000 until the 19C. The old Cathedral, founded in the earliest centuries of Christianity, was smaller and simpler than the present-day one. It was transformed into a mosque during Arab rule but was restored to the Christian cult in 1072, after the liberation of the city by the army of the Hauteville brothers. The rather decayed Cathedral, however, was further damaged by earthquakes, so much so that, after the earthquake of 1169, Bishop Gualtiero II ordered that it should be reconstructed as a more majestic and sumptuous building. This was meant to confirm the supremacy of the Pope in Rome as the feudal Lord of the Sicilian kingdom, and the supremacy of the Latin confession over the Byzantine, but also to house the increasing masses of newly converted believers, mostly Berbers and Arabs. The magnificent new construction also housed the porphyry sarcophagi of the sovereigns of Sicily,

but remained unfinished at the death of Bishop Gualtiero. Work for its completion was carried on, albeit discontinuously, in the 13C and 14C, but the planned dome was not constructed at that time. Only in the 15C was the sumptuous south triple-arched portico, which is still the main entrance to the Cathedral, accomplished. Gagini's imposing Retablo was mounted in the 16C but dismantled at the end of the 18C. In the 17C an extensive renovation project was blocked by the

Canons of the Cathedral. However, the sumptuous Chapel of St Rosalia, entirely decorated with marble inlaid work, was created to house the precious silver urn containing the remains of the city's patron saint. The Chapel was later dismantled and reconstructed in its present position, near the transept, while another chapel was built along the south aisle to house the urns with the remains of the former patron saints of the city: St Agatha, St Christine, St Ninfa and St Oliva. Finally, between 1781 and 1801, extensive renovation work was carried out which completely transformed the original medieval aspect of the Cathedral – particularly its interior – in accordance with Neoclassical aesthetic taste. The project was drawn up by the royal architect Ferdinando Fuga, although the architects who directed the building site carried out further alterations on their own initiative. The nave and aisles were shortened; the transept area was completely transformed, and the present-day dome was built. The overall result did not appeal to many Palermitans and aroused great controversy. Today, evocative visits can be made to the Crypt, which houses the sarcophagi of numerous Bishops of Palermo, and to the Chapel of the Royal Tombs, where the porphyry sarcophagi of some of the greatest European sovereigns are to be found, namely those of King Roger II of Hauteville, Constance of Hauteville, wife of Henry VI and mother of Frederick II, Henry VI Hohenstaufen and Frederick II Hohenstaufen. Set into a wall is also the sarcophagus of Constance of Aragon, the first wife of Frederick II. The close contact between the sovereigns of Sicily and the Cathedral is underlined by the fact that they were all crowned in this Cathedral with magnificent ceremonies, and that many of them celebrated their sumptuous weddings and were buried here.

Opposite page, top: Palermo. Cathedral. South front looking onto the square.
Opposite page, bottom: Palermo. Cathedral. South triple-arched portico, a masterpiece of Palermo's 15C architectural syncretism.

Above: Palermo. Cathedral. The porphyry sarcophagus of Frederick II also contains the remains of two other historical personages. Built in the 12C for King Roger II, the sarcophagus remained empty for a long time, until it was chosen by Frederick II as his own tomb.

IMPERIAL TOMBS

Palermo Cathedral houses a treasure of outstanding historical value which is the envy of most of the world. In fact, the sumptuous porphyry sarcophagi of some of the greatest European medieval sovereigns are to be found in a chapel of the south aisle. These monumental tombs were actually ordered by King Roger II of Hauteville for himself and his family in the 12C. They were placed in the Duomo of Cefalù as the sovereign wanted this church to be a mausoleum for the Hauteville royal family. But due to a series of adverse circumstances, his plan failed. Roger II was buried in Palermo Cathedral, in a temporary sarcophagus consisting of reused porphyry slabs where he still lies. In the 13C Emperor Frederick II Hohenstaufen resolved to move the sarcophagi of the Hauteville family from Cefalù to Palermo Cathedral, where he earmarked them for himself, his father Henry VI and his mother Constance of Hauteville. For his wife, Constance of Aragon, he chose an ancient Roman sarcophagus (now set into a wall of the chapel). The 12C porphyry sarcophagi are extraordinary – indeed unique – works of art. Their uniqueness stems, to begin with, from the material used, as Egyptian red porphyry was a Roman and Byzantine imperial prerogative on account of its hardness, great value, and of the skill necessary to work it. Then, from their form, which is high, with the lower portion resembling the keel of a boat.

THE ZISA

One of the masterpieces of Sicilian medieval architecture (12C) this is the most important and famous of a series of royal *domus*, designed as pleasure residences for the Sicilian sovereigns. These palaces (Zisa, Cuba Soprana, Cuba Sottana, Parco-Altofonte, Favara-Maredolce, and others) were built within the magnificent Royal Park situated just outside the city walls, a large woodland area which was at the same time a game reserve where Palermitan monarchs would go hunting, fishing, relaxing or meeting their friends and mistresses. On the upper edge of the building, a Cufic inscription extols the figure of King Roger II of Hauteville and defines the palace *Aziz* (Splendid), hence the name *Zisa*. The palace was built between 1164 and 1180 by craftsmen from the Maghreb. The lower portion was ordered by William I, while the upper portion was built by his son William II. Before the entrance there used to be an artificial lake, traces of which are still visible today. On the ground floor is the *iwan*, a large room with three exedrae covered by vaults, of remote Anatolian-Persian origin, where a fountain set against the wall supplied water to a small artificial stream. On the first floor is a "Hall of the Winds", a roofless terrace surrounded by a portico. The interior was pleasantly ventilated thanks to a system of ventiducts in the walls. The palace also had functional sanitary facilities.

Opposite page, top: Palermo. Zisa (a Domus). Façade.

Opposite page, bottom: Palermo. Zisa. The iwan room with its small fountain.

THE CAPUCHIN CATACOMBS

The crypts of the Capuchin Monastery, built in 1621, house the world-famous "Capuchin Catacombs".

This macabre place contains the mummified or embalmed bodies of some eight thousand wealthy Palermitans (including women and children) and clergymen, who were buried there until 1881, when the custom was abolished.

In the adjoining graveyard is the tomb of G. Tomasi di Lampedusa, author of the famous novel "The Leopard".

THE CUBA

This peculiar building was built by King William II of Hauteville in 1180, within the boundaries of the great Royal Park situated outside the city walls. Its structure partly reflects the *domus* model of the Zisa, particularly in its height. Unlike the Zisa, however, the building consists of only three rooms situated on the same floor. A small vestibule at the entrance leads into a large roofless courtyard, formerly surrounded by a portico. This in turn leads into a large *iwan*. The fact that the building was surrounded by an artificial lake, that its original entrance is very small, and that its high walls are pierced by small windows but only from some height upwards suggests a strong desire for privacy. In fact, according to the specialist in medieval architecture Rodo Santoro, this was probably the building where the Palermitan sovereigns spent their time with their mistresses.

Top: Palermo. Mummified bodies in the "Capuchin Catacombs".

Left: Palermo. Cuba (a Domus).

CHURCH OF SAN GIOVANNI DEI LEBBROSI

During the Saracen rule, the site was occupied by a small fort which was seized by the army of the Hauteville brothers, Robert "the Guiscard" and Roger I, Great Count of Sicily, prior to their conquest of the city in 1072. Shortly afterwards Roger decided to build the church as a way of thanking God for his victory. In fact, this was probably the first Christian church to have been erected in Palermo after the restoration of the city to the Christian cult at the end of almost one and a half centuries of Saracen rule. This accounts for its bare, simple yet strongly suggestive interior. In 1150 the old fort was used as a leper hospital, hence the name of the church (St John of the Lepers), but no traces have remained of the building. The church is roughly oblong in plan, with a nave and two aisles divided by pillars without capitals, and three apses in the Byzantine style. The centre of the short transept is covered by a hemispherical dome resting on a drum. The upper

Above: Palermo. Church of San Giovanni dei Lebbrosi.

portion of the front and the bell tower are modern (1934).

CHURCH OF SANTA MARIA DELL'AMMIRAGLIO: THE "MARTORANA"

Erected around 1143 as a Palace Chapel by George of Antioch, Grand Admiral to King Roger II of Hauteville, the building was originally conceived as a central-plan church (a Greek cross inscribed

in a square), hence as a typical medieval Byzantine church with a central dome and three apses facing east. Craftsmen from the Maghreb also contributed to its construction. The internal walls were entirely covered with magnificent, glittering Byzantine mosaics (12C), mostly reflecting the dedication of the church to the Virgin Mary. Two mosaic panels – separate from the others – depict respectively the Grand Admiral kneeling down before the Virgin Mary and Roger II crowned by Christ in accordance with the imperial Byzantine tradition. After the foundation, in 1194, of the nearby Benedictine convent of the Martorana, to which the church was adjoined, the interior had to be transformed to be adapted to the Latin rite, which replaced the Greek one. The original central plan was completely altered between the 16C and 17C, when the nave and aisles were considerably lengthened and the women's gallery was built. The monumental baroque front looking onto present-day Piazza Bellini was also completed. The vaults of the new spaces were richly decorated with frescoes by skilled painters of the time, contributing to the sumptuous aspect of the church. The building, as we see it today, is the most extraordinary example of Byzantine-Latin religious and aesthetic culture in Sicily, characterized by the mystical and fascinating atmosphere of its gold mosaics, including the famous *Nativity* and *Dormition of the Virgin*. The church, originally known as Santa Maria dell'Ammiraglio, became known as the "Martorana" from the nearby Latin convent to which it was adjoined. It is now dedicated to St Nicholas of Myra to mark its continuity with the former parish of Palermitans who observed the Byzantine rite, and is also the sister Cathedral of the Byzantine Eparchy of Piana degli Albanesi. Suggestive rites are celebrated in the church, including weddings with bride and groom dressed in the traditional Albanian costumes, christenings by immersion in water, and the Byzantine Easter celebrations.

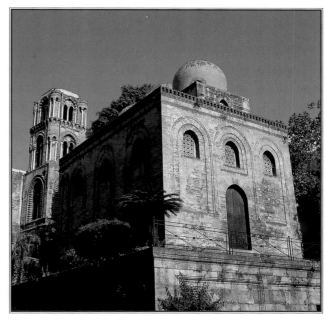

*Above: Palermo.
Church of San Cataldo.*

CHURCH OF SAN CATALDO

This small church was built around 1160 by Maio of Bari, Grand Chancellor to King William I of Hauteville and one of the greatest statesmen of the 12C, as a private chapel in his palace (no longer extant). The peculiar architectural structure of the building is unique in Palermo and Sicily. It may be compared to a rectangular prism, covered by three small cupolas which follow the longitudinal axis of the building. This type of structure is also present in numerous small Byzantine churches of medieval Apulia and Cyprus. A similar-style church is to be found at Ognissanti di Cuti, near Bari, on a site which was once part of Maio's family estate. The difference between the small Apulian churches covered by three cupolas and San Cataldo, however, consists in a number of architectural features which, in the latter, were constructed by craftsmen from the Maghreb. The exterior, for example, is characterized by high blind arches framing small ogival windows. The unadorned, charming interior has maintained its original medieval atmosphere.

*Opposite page, bottom:
Palermo. Church of Santa
Maria dell'Ammiraglio
(Martorana). Bell tower and
central apse.*

Palermo. Fontana delle Vergogne in Piazza Pretoria. The sumptuously scenic design of the fountain is enhanced by the buildings in the background.

PIAZZA PRETORIA AND FONTANA DELLE VERGOGNE

This is one of the most scenic squares in the old city centre. It was named after the Town Hall ("Pretorio"), which is also called "Palazzo delle Aquile" (the Palace of the Eagles), one of the prestigious buildings which mark the boundaries of the square together with two outstanding religious buildings facing one another on its east and west sides. On the east side is the *Church of Santa Caterina*, built between 1580 and 1596 in late-Renaissance style, and adjoined to an important Dominican monastery. The imposing dome dates from the mid-18C. On the west side of the monumental square is the east front of the *Church of San Giuseppe dei Teatini*, surmounted by the delicate dome covered with polychrome majolica tiles and resting on a drum decorated with twin columns. Designed by the Theatine friar Giacomo Besio, the church was begun in 1612 and completed in 1645. The magnificent circular fountain which occupies almost the entire square is the work of the Florentine architect Francesco Camillani. Originally designed for the Florentine villa of Don Pedro of Toledo, it was sold back to the city of Palermo in 1573.

THE SICILIAN REGIONAL GALLERY AT "PALAZZO ABATELLIS" AND THE "ANTONIO SALINAS" ARCHAEOLOGICAL MUSEUM

The Regional Gallery is housed in Palazzo Abatellis, built in 1490-95 by Matteo Carnelivari in late Gothic-Catalan forms with Renaissance influences. The sumptuous residence was commissioned by Francesco Abatellis, a royal "pretore" (magistrate) of Palermo, and his wife Eleonora Soler. Seriously damaged during World War II, the building was restored in 1954 by Carlo Scarpa. Its rooms house an important collection of sculptures and paintings by renowned Sicilian and European artists, particularly from the 14C and 16C. The entrance and courtyard rooms display sculptures from different periods and by different artists, as well as statues, stonework and pottery, architectural fragments and the coat of arms of the Abatellis and of other Sicilian noble families.

Above: Palermo. Regional Gallery. Fresco of the "Triumph of Death", formerly in Palazzo Sclafani (anon., 15C).
Left: Regional Gallery. Statue of Madonna and Child, a splendid example of the elegance and grace which characterize the Madonnas sculpted by Antonello Gagini (1478-1536).

The Gallery has sixteen exhibition rooms which alternately display masterpieces of painting and sculpture, including the works of *Francesco Laurana, Antonello da Messina, Antonello Gagini* and his school, *Domenico Gagini, Serpotta* and other famous artists.

With its vast collection of Greek and Roman works, the Regional Archaeological Museum is one of the foremost archaeological museums in Italy.

It is housed in the *former Olivella monastery*, adjoining the Church of Sant'Ignazio all'Olivella, built between 1598 and 1622 to a design by Antonio Muttone, with a magnificent 17C baroque façade adorned with three portals. The exhibition rooms are arranged on the three floors of the former Monastery of the Congregation of St Philip, and feature archaeological finds, masterpieces of sculpture, collections of vases, coins and epigraphs that span the millennia, from the Phoenician civilization to the Greek colonization and the Roman Age, testifying to Sicily's noble past.

*Above:
Palermo. Archaeological Museum. Entrance courtyard, Fountain of Triton (16C).*

*Right:
Archaeological Museum. Bronze ram (3C BC) from Syracuse. Together with its pair, it once decorated the portal of the Maniace Castle in Syracuse and was later moved to the Royal Palace in Palermo.*

Archaeological Museum. Bronze youth from Selinunte (Siceliot work, 480 BC).

THE CHIARAMONTE FAMILY'S "STERI" PALACE

The peculiar name of this medieval building derives from the Latin *Hosterium* (Hostel), used to indicate the residence of an aristocratic family, which did not only consist of the family's house and reception halls, but also included workshops, stables, warehouses, to form a truly self-sufficient complex. The majestic "Steri" palace was built between 1306 and 1392 on the orders of Giovanni Chiaramonte "the Elder". Although the upper floor was left unfinished, it became the largest aristocratic residence in Palermo. In 1392 the last lord of the Chiaramonte family, Andrea, accused of rebellion against the Crown, was beheaded in the square below the palace. The building later became the residence of the viceroys and then the seat of the Court of the Holy Office. It was the seat of the Civil Courts until World War II and finally, after restoration work carried out in the second half of the 20C, it became the seat of the Rectorate of Palermo University. The building is characterized by a massive structure, externally decorated with magnificent three-light windows. The internal courtyard features a solemn lower portico and an elegant upper loggia. Rooms of different dimensions are arranged along its square perimeter. Two large rooms, one on the first and the other on the second floor, reflect the political power of the Chiaramonte family. The room on the first floor is covered by the richest and most magnificent wooden ceiling of the Sicilian 14C, entirely decorated with exquisite paintings depicting scenes of chivalry and ancient myths which make up one of the greatest pictorial cycles of the late Middle Ages. Adjoining the palace is the small medieval church of Sant'Antonino Abate (perhaps the Chiaramonte family's Chapel), and the 17C "Jail of Penance", where Inquisition prisoners were held. Wall paintings, drawings and graffiti can still be seen in some of the cells.

Above:
Palermo. The Chiaramonte family's Steri palace, now housing the Rectorate of Palermo University.

GIACOMO SERPOTTA (1656 – 1732)

Together with a host of relatives (Gaspare, Giovan Maria, Giuseppe, Procopio) and collaborators, and as well as being a marble sculptor, Giacomo Serpotta was the most outstanding figure of the decorative plastic arts between the 17C and 18C (stuccoes and gessoes). The heir of a long-established Palermitan tradition – which went back as far as the Middle Ages – he brought his art to the height of virtuosity and formal elegance, outclassing the European production of the time. His

Palermo. Oratory of the Rosario near the Church of Santa Cita. The Battle of Lepanto.

25

Palermo. Church of San Matteo, interior. Fresco in the vault depicting "The Triumph of the Souls in Purgatory" by Vito D'Anna (1754).

plastic compositions are crowded with putti and female figures. The peculiar "soft-skin" effect in these figures was obtained by means of a special technique of stucco preparation which made the skin surfaces appear almost ethereal – and which remained a professional secret of this family of artists for a long time. The production of Serpotta's workshop was vast and can still be admired in the following churches: Carmine Maggiore, del Gesù, Sant'Agostino, Sant'Anna la Misericordia, San Domenico, San Francesco d'Assisi, Santa Maria degli Angeli, Santa Maria del Giusino, Santa Maria di Monte Oliveto, Santa Maria della Pietà, San Matteo, Santa Ninfa dei Crociferi, Sant'Orsola, San Sebastiano, Collegio Massimo dei Padri Gesuiti. The decorative ensembles for the Oratories of the Confraternities are also famous: the Oratories of San Francesco di Paola ai Candelai, of the Rosario in Santa Cita and San Domenico, of San Lorenzo, San Mercurio and Santissimi Pietro e Paolo.

PIETRO NOVELLI AND VITO D'ANNA

Pietro Novelli is the greatest Sicilian painter of the 17C. He was influenced by Caravaggio's style of art, Neapolitan painting of the time and Van Dyck. Frescoes and paintings from his vast artistic production can still be admired in several Palermitan churches, in spite of the damage and losses caused by bombings during World War II. He was also an architect and designer of *festival machines*. The following churches contain works by Pietro Novelli: San Giuseppe dei Teatini, Sant'Ignazio all'Olivella, Santa Maria degli Angeli, Santa Maria di Monte Oliveto, San Matteo, San Nicolò da Tolentino, Sant'Orsola.

Vito D'Anna (1718-1769) is considered to be the greatest Palermitan fresco painter of the 18C. His painting was characterized by bold perspective compositions, an airy style, clear and brilliant colours. His vast production was mainly concerned with the decoration of vaults in aristocratic palaces and churches in Palermo. His most important works are to be found in the following buildings: Palazzo Termine di Isnello, Palazzo Termine-Marassi di Pietratagliata, Villa Filippina, Villa Napoli, Villa Resuttano-Terrasi, as well as in the following churches: Sant'Anna la Misericordia, Sant'Antonio Abate, Santa Caterina, San Francesco d'Assisi, San Francesco di Paola, Santa Maria del Piliere, San Matteo, Santissimo Salvatore, San Sebastiano, Tre Re.

TEATRO POLITEAMA GARIBALDI

The theatre was originally also conceived as a masonry arena for circuses and covered with a movable cupola. It was built between 1867 and 1874 to a design by Giuseppe Damiani Almeyda, the fierce rival of G. B. F. Basile (who designed the Teatro Massimo), in a vaguely Classical style. The curved façade features a lower portico and upper ambulatory, with a double order of Doric and Ionic columns. It is interrupted, in the middle, by the protruding entrance portal in the style of a Roman triumphal arch, surmounted by a bronze quadriga with pawing horses flanked by two genii on horseback, sculpted by Mario Rutelli.

Above: Palermo.
Teatro Politeama G. Garibaldi and (left) detail of the bronze quadriga above the entrance portal (sculpted by M. Rutelli).

TEATRO MASSIMO

The theatre is one of the architectural masterpieces of Italian Neoclassicism and one of the largest opera houses in Europe, ranking third in proscenium size after the *Opéra* in Paris and the *Opernhaus* in Vienna. It was designed by Giovan Battista Filippo Basile, the greatest Palermitan architect of the 19C, who also directed its construction. This was begun in 1875 but completed by his son Ernesto, the leading figure of the *Liberty* style (Italian *Art Nouveau*). The theatre has a covered surface area of 7,730 sq m, with a vast and sumptuous auditorium covering 450 sq m. It has a total seating capacity of 3,200 including auditorium seats, five tiers of boxes and a gallery. The magnificent decorations are the work of a host of Palermitan artists including the sculptors B. Civiletti, M. Rutelli and A. Ugo. The huge stage curtain depicts Roger II of Sicily parading on the day of his coronation as the first king of Sicily, by G. Sciuti.

Palermo. Teatro Massimo. Façade looking onto Piazza Verdi. One of the greatest opera houses in the world, it is the masterpiece of the architect Giovan Battista Filippo Basile. His son, the architect Ernesto Basile, was to become one of the masters of European Art Nouveau.

Above:
Palermo. Palazzina Cinese.

Centre: Palermo.
Palazzina Cinese, interior.

PALAZZINA CINESE

Situated within the great Royal Park, now known as "La Favorita", this peculiar building was designed by the royal architect Venanzio Marvuglia and built in 1799 for the Bourbon king Ferdinand IV. Its bizarre architecture is a combination of different styles, including Gothic and neo-classical elements enriched with Chinese-like motifs. During King Ferdinand IV's stay in Palermo, this palace became the pleasure residence of the sovereign and his wife Maria Carolina. The walls and vaults of the interiors were decorated with frescoes by G. Patania and V. Riolo. The ballroom and the royal audience hall, in Louis XVI style, are on the ground floor. On the first floor is the reception hall and the dining room, where the table has an ingenious mechanical device which allowed dishes to be served without the intrusion of servants into the rooms. On the left side of the building is the Royal Chapel, in neoclassical style, octagonal in plan and covered by a cupola resting on eight Ionic marble columns.

Opposite page:
Palermo. Ethnographic Museum.

Top: The annexe to the Palazzina Cinese which houses the Museum.

Centre: Portrait of Giuseppe Pitrè. Engraving by G. Vuillier (late 19C).

Bottom: Marionette of the Puppet Theatre.

THE "GIUSEPPE PITRÈ" SICILIAN ETHNOGRAPHIC MUSEUM

This is one of the most famous ethnographic museums in Italy. It is the property of the Palermo Municipality and was created in 1909 by the great ethnographer Giuseppe Pitrè, the founder of the Italian school of folk psychology. Since 1935 the museum has been housed in the pavilions adjoining the Palazzina Cinese, in the Favorita Park. It displays the largest existing collection of items related to Sicilian "popular" life and culture, providing the most comprehensive documentation of the usage, customs, beliefs, myths, habits and traditions of the Sicilian people. The museum collections contain about 4,000 items, including 1,500 which were part of Pitrè's original collection, items from the ethnographic collections of the former Palermo National Museum, and others donated by private citizens. The items are displayed in 30 rooms, divided into 15 sections which have essentially maintained the layout designed by Giuseppe Cocchiara, a distinguished scientist and disciple of Pitrè.

The first section is dedicated to rural and urban dwelling places, from straw huts to the houses of the *burgisi* (members of the middle class). The following sections are related to hunting and fishing, agriculture and sheep-farming, costumes, carvings and pieces of pottery, magic and religion, toys, feasts and shows, carts. A puppet theatre has been set up in one room, with various puppets (Angelica, Orlando, Morgante, Rinaldo) and posters depicting the scenes which the *Pupara* (puppeteers) represent on the stage. Then there is the room dedicated to the Sicilian cart, with models showing the different stages of production, and the Christmas crib room, including works by unknown artists and by Giovanni Matera (a famous 18C potter). More than 300 statuettes represent the Nativity and the Slaughter of the Innocents. Other interesting rooms contain the coaches of the ancient Palermitan Senate, and models, drawings and prints of the most notable Triumphal Chariots of St Rosalia created in the 19C-20C. There is also a fine collection of *ex-votos*, including paintings on wood, tin-plate and canvas, each depicting the miracle experienced by the donor

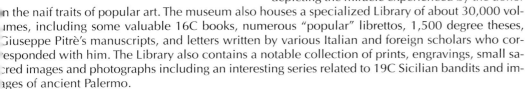

n the naif traits of popular art. The museum also houses a specialized Library of about 30,000 volumes, including some valuable 16C books, numerous "popular" librettos, 1,500 degree theses, Giuseppe Pitrè's manuscripts, and letters written by various Italian and foreign scholars who corresponded with him. The Library also contains a notable collection of prints, engravings, small sacred images and photographs including an interesting series related to 19C Sicilian bandits and images of ancient Palermo.

Palermo. Mount Pellegrino. Sanctuary of St Rosalia. Top: Interior of the cave. Above: Exterior.

THE SANCTUARY OF SANTA ROSALIA

The veneration of the Palermitan people for their *Santuzza*, as they call St Rosalia, the patron saint of the city, can be traced back to the 12C but took on impressive proportions after the plague epidemic of 1624. In those terrible days, a number of believers began digging in a cave on Mount Pellegrino, where Rosalia had lived her last years as a hermit, and did not stop until they found her bones. But who was Rosalia? Born in 1132, the daughter of Count Sinibaldo della Quisquinia and Mary Guiscard (a relative of King Roger II), when still a young girl she was introduced to court as a lady-in-waiting to Queen Margaret of Navarre, the wife of King William I, known as "the Bad". When her father fell into disgrace, perhaps as a consequence of his support for the anti-royal revolt led by Matteo Bonello (1161), the young Rosalia was forced to leave the court and resolved to go and live as a hermit in Quisquinia, where her family had a fief. Later, she moved to a cave on Mount Pellegrino, where she died on 4 September 1166. She was proclaimed a saint soon after her death, and her popular cult flourished to the point that crowds of barefoot pilgrims would climb Mount Pellegrino and spend the night near the cave where she had lived her hermit's life. Since then, a similar pilgrimage has taken place every 4 September. After the official identification, her bones were carried in procession through the city on 15 July 1625. The plague epidemic subsided and finally ended, and St Rosalia was proclaimed the main patron saint of the city.

MONDELLO

The Palermitan beach resort *par excellence*, Mondello nestles in the delightful bay between Mount Pellegrino and Mount Gallo. The site was formerly a vast swampy region of deep brackish waters extending from the sea up to the plain further inland. Later, it became the favourite place for hunting and fishing of the Bourbon king Ferdinand IV. The area was finally reclaimed at the beginning of the 20C, and today Mondello is one of the best-known bathing resorts in Sicily. Since the post-war period it has become increasingly popular and has experienced considerable urban development which, however, has spared the extensive green areas that surround the private villas. Hotels and recreation facilities have also been built. The site, which still deserves the name of a "garden town", has attracted many Palermitans who have chosen to live here, far from Palermo's busy traffic. The older inhabited nucleus (a fishing village) lies at the north end of the bay, on the site of an ancient tunny-fishery whose 15C round tower is still visible. A watchtower of the same period stands aloof on the furthermost rocky spur to the west of the bay. At the beginning of the 20C, when the *Belle Epoque* was at its height, the first elite residences were built, followed by many others throughout the period between the two wars. Of great interest are Villa Dagnino (1914), Villa Pojero (1915) and the Sea *Kursaal* (bathing establishment), built in the late-floral style in fashion at the time.

Palermo. Mondello. Panoramic view from Mount Pellegrino.

USTICA

Almost in the centre of the lower Tyrrhenian Sea, 57 km from Palermo, lies the small island o Ustica, whose name means "oyster". The island, which has for some years now attracted a grow ing number of visitors, is elliptical in shape (2.7 x 4.5 km) and covers an area of 8.6 sq km. Of vol canic origin, prevalently composed of black lava rock, it is, however, covered with a rich vegeta tion and its products include wheat, eggs and fruit. The sea abounds in fish. Ustica has had a tormented history: it was frequently ravaged by pirates, and its population was deported on sev eral occasions, first by the Saracens and then by the Barbary pirates. Only in 1763 did the Bourbons build blockhouses and watchtowers, established a garrison of 250 soldiers to defend the island and repopulated it with some hundred families. Today Ustica is linked to Palermo by regular ship and hydrofoil services and is an ideal destination for fascinating holidays far from the chaos of city life Its incomparable underwater seascapes, in particular, attract a large number of lovers of underwate sports and activities. In fact, Ustica is the seat of the famous "International Festival of Underwate Activities". The presence of small hotels and the possibility to rent houses from the local popula tion also make the island an ideal holiday resort for families.

Ustica. The small town. Overlooking the town, on the left, is one of the watchtowers of the island.

*Palermo. Festino of St Rosalia.
The statue of the Santuzza on
the Triumphal Chariot.*

*Triumphal Chariot of
St Rosalia designed by
Don Paolo Amato for the
Festino of 1701.*

THE "FESTINO" OF SANTA ROSALIA

The virgin Rosalia lived in the 12C, during the reign of William I of Hauteville, known as "the Bad". She was of noble descent and when a young girl she was a lady-in-waiting to Queen Margaret of Navarre. Disgusted with life at court, she resolved to lead a hermit's life, first on the Mount of Quisquinia, then on Mount

Festino of St Rosalia. "Flying Angels" at Porta Felice.

Below: Festino of St Rosalia. "Firework display" in the Marina promenade.

Opposite page, top: Duomo of Monreale. West front with the two towers.

Opposite page, bottom: Monreale. Panoramic view of the town and of the Conca d'Oro plain.

Pellegrino. She was canonized Saint soon after her death, and her popular cult flourished to the point that her heavenly intervention was invoked during plague epidemics and earthquakes. During the plague epidemic of 1624 believers found her bones in the cave on Mount Pellegrino where she had lived her hermit life. After the official identification of the bones, the plague epidemic subsided and finally ended. The bones were put in a magnificent silver urn and carried in procession through the city. Since then (1625), a similar procession has taken place every year and more solemn and sumptuous forms of celebration have been introduced, which have transformed the festival into the most important religious and lay event in Palermo, known as the "Festino". In the 17C-18C the city Senate introduced a procession of allegoric carts which preceded a magnificent Triumphal Chariot drawn by several horses and characterized by the presence of an orchestra. This "machine" symbolized the glorious triumph of the *Santuzza*, as Palermitans affectionately call their patron saint. In the first half of the 19C the smaller carts were abolished and the Triumphal Chariot was made increasingly large and more sumptuous. The annual construction of the Chariot was interrupted in 1860, then resumed in 1896-97 (by the ethnographer Giuseppe Pitrè) and again in 1924. The tradition has now continued uninterrupted since 1974. Although the duration of the festival may vary from year to year, its climax is always on 15 July. It should be pointed out, however, that to be precise the "Festino" is not the festival of the patron saint of the city, but rather a feast of thanksgiving for having escaped the plague. On 4 September the Palermitans celebrate the *dies natalis* (death in sanctity) of St Rosalia with the traditional *acchianata* (climb) up Mount Pellegrino, i.e. the pilgrimage of believers – barefoot and holding candles in their hands – to the sanctuary built in the Saint's cave.

DUOMO OF MONREALE
"The most beautiful Temple in the world"

The Duomo stands at the edge of the historical centre of Monreale, a small town overlooking the Oreto River valley and the famous Conca d'Oro plain. Referred to as "The golden temple", a fairy-tale construction, it was the Christian apotheosis dreamt by a king, William II of Hauteville, known as "the Good", the grandson of King Roger II and third sovereign of the Kingdom of Sicily. To fully understand the reasons why, at the end of the 12C, this king promoted the construction of the majestic architectural complex at Monreale, financed by the Royal Treasury, it is necessary to recall the political and religious relations which existed at the time between the Kingdom of Sicily and the Pope in Rome. The Sicilian State was, in fact, a vassal state of the Pope because it had been established by a political resolution of the Pope himself, who had also granted the Palermitan sovereigns the privilege of appointing the Latin bishops of the Kingdom. This procedure, however, made the bishops to some extent submis-

sive to the king, the only exception being the Bishop of Palermo, who was appointed by the Canons of the Cathedral and represented the Pope at court. The Hautevilles made several attempts to gain greater autonomy vis-à-vis the political authority of the Pope. One of these was the creation, at Monreale, of a Bishopric loyal to the Crown, which extended its jurisdiction over a larger territory than that of the Bishopric of Palermo. In 1174, at the early age of 20, the king began the construction of the Duomo and of the great architectural complex including the Benedictine Abbey, the Archbishop's Palace and the Royal Palace. The design of the Duomo combines the Latin-cross basilican plan with a Byzantine-type square sanctuary. The church is not domed and covers a vast

*Duomo of Monreale.
The nave and, at the far end,
the transept and the central
apse.*

*Below: Duomo of Monreale.
The three apses facing east.*

area (102 m long and 40 m wide). It is divided into a nave and two aisles by two rows of nine columns each, with capitals of exquisite workmanship (*clypei* of pagan divinities, acanthus leaves and cornucopias overflowing with fruit) surmounted by mosaic-covered pulvinoes (Byzantine transformation of the Greek abacus). The columns bear pointed arches in the Fatimide style. The mosaic floor features granite and porphyry geometric decorations. The walls of the nave, transept and apses are en-

Duomo of Monreale.
Byzantine mosaics (12C).
Top: Christ Pantocrator (the
Lord of the Universe).

Bottom, left: William II
dressed as a Byzantine
"Basileus", presenting a
model of the Duomo to the
Virgin Mary.
Bottom, right: William II
crowned by Christ in
accordance with the official
Byzantine iconography.

tirely covered with mosaics on a gilded background, covering a total surface area of 6,340 sq m. The work of Byzantine craftsmen, they were completed between the 12C and 13C and depict a cycle of scenes from the Old and New Testaments. The design and the direction of the work were certainly entrusted to Benedictine monks from Campania. The masons employed were those who, a few years before, had arrived in Palermo from the Maghreb territories conquered by Admiral George of Antioch on behalf of King Roger II. Master mosaicists were summoned from Greece, while the hand of Campanian and Apulian artists can be seen in many sculptural decorative motifs. In short, the construction involved builders, craftsmen, artists and workers from various areas of the vast territory ruled by the Kingdom of Sicily in the 12C. In order to somehow account for the great expenditure incurred in the building of the monumental complex at Monreale, a legend was circulated: William II was said to have been resting during a shooting party on the hill of Monreale, when he dreamt of the Virgin Mary, who showed him a hidden treasure which, however, was to be used for the construction of a great church dedicated to her.

BENEDICTINE CLOISTER

This splendid example of Sicilian Romanesque architecture and sculpture was built by King William II together with the basilica and the Benedictine monastery of which it was part. Square in plan, it covers an area of 47 x 47 m and is surrounded by a portico with an uninterrupted series of 228 small paired columns bearing capitals and pointed arches. This is what a remarkable visitor from the 19C, the writer and novelist Guy de Maupassant, wrote about the cloister in his "Journey to Sicily": *"The marvellous Monreale cloister, instead, conjures up an impression of such grace as to make one want to stay there forever… The exquisite proportions, the incredible slenderness of the light paired columns, one beside the other, all different, some covered with mosaics, others bare; some decorated with sculptures of unmatched delicacy, others adorned with simple stone carvings which wind round them as a creeper would, are a wonder to behold, casting spells and generating that artistic joy which, through the eye,*

penetrates the soul at the sight of such exquisite beauty. How could one not love these cloisters, so steeped in peace, secluded and created, it might seem, with the express purpose of generating most profound thoughts as one walks slowly beneath the arcades! How one feels that these corridors of stone, these corridors of columns enclosing a small garden which rests the eye without disturbing or distracting it, were created to stir one's imagination!".

Benedictine Cloister.
Top: Overall view. The Cloister is a refined blend of 12C architecture, sculpture and decorative arts.
Above: Capital depicting William II in the act of presenting a model of the Duomo to the Virgin Mary.

CASTLE OF CACCAMO

The largest feudal castle in Sicily, it stands in a picturesque position on the western slopes of Mount Calogero, in the mountainous area behind the town of Termini Imerese. Solid and compact in appearance, it consists of several constructions dating from various ages, from the 11C to the 17C, perched on different levels of a rock overlooking the town centre and the San Leonardo valley, now filled by the waters of an artificial lake. Originally a small fortress, it was enlarged first by the Chiaramonte family in the 14C, then by the Prades-Cabrera family in the 15C, and finally by the Amato family in the 17C. At present it is the property of the Sicilian Region. A long flight of stairs (17C) leads to the central courtyard. The interior features rooms of various sizes and importance, including a large stable and a spacious audience hall (in the Prades Wing), as well as magnificent 17C halls in the Amato Wing. The ancient prisons still retain their original dismal appearance. Restoration work carried out in the 20C (by the last owners, the Galati-de Spuches family, and then by the Region) has made the building suitable for hosting conferences and exhibitions.

*Castle of Caccamo (11C-17C).
Below: Caccamo. General
view of the Castle and town.*

CASTLE OF CASTELBUONO

This was for centuries the manor house of the Ventimiglia family, one of the most important aristocratic families in Sicily. Recent restoration work has brought to light – in the basement of the castle – the massive architectural structures of a royal "*castrum*" dating from the end of the 13C, with numerous large arrow slits. Upon these structures, in 1316, the Ventimiglia built their feudal residence. In the 15C the castle was renovated and its upper part built. A chapel was also created to house a most important relic, the skull of St Anne. In the 17C the chapel was moved to a different position, and enriched with a sumptuous baroque stucco decoration, the work of the Palermitan Serpotta family, the greatest stucco decorators of the 17C in Italy. The Great Hall features a wooden ceiling carved and painted according to the Sicilian late-medieval tradition. Today the castle is the property of the Castelbuono Municipality. It houses a large number of archaeological and architectural finds. St Anne's Chapel – now a Sanctuary – still attracts believers from all the towns and villages in the Madonie mountains.

Above: Castle of Castelbuono.

Below: The town of Castelbuono and its impressive Castle.

Above:
Cefalù Cathedral.

Centre:
Cefalù Cathedral.
The splendid Byzantine
mosaic of Christ Pantocrator.

Bottom: Cefalù.
The majestic Cathedral
dominating the town.

Opposite page, top: Cefalù.
Mandralisca Museum.
Graeco-Siceliot bell-shaped
crater from Lipari (4C BC)

Opposite page, bottom:
Cefalù. Mandralisca Museum.
"Portrait of an Unknown
Man" by Antonello da
Messina (1430-1479).

CEFALÙ

The ancient name of the town, *Kephaloidion*, derived from the Greek *kefalè* (headland, promontory) and referred to the promontory overlooking the present-day urban area. The area was inhabited in prehistoric times, as is confirmed by the traces of human settlements in the caves on the slopes of the promontory. In pre-Hellenic times the site was probably used as a trading post by the Phoenicians from the west of the island and by Greek colonists from the east. The most reliable historical data on Cefalù are provided by Diodorus and refer back to 396 BC, when the Carthaginian general Himilco entered into an alliance with its population. It was later occupied by Dionysius, a tyrant of Syracuse. In 307 BC, under the terms of the agreement made with Carthage, it was conquered by Agathocles, a general and tyrant of Syracuse born at Himera. In 254 BC it was conquered by the Romans following betrayal by a faction of its citizens. It then became a Roman *civitas decumana* and enjoyed a period of prosperity. In 858 AD Cefalù put up a lengthy resistance to Saracen attacks, but it was eventually burnt and its population slaughtered. A period of great splendour began for the town in the 12C, when King Roger II of Hauteville built the great Cathedral (which he intended to be a mausoleum for his family), the Royal Palace and new boundary walls. An impressive castle surrounded by walls was erected at the top of the promontory, known as the "Rocca", traces of which are still visible today. Over the following centuries the political prestige of the Bishop of Cefalù increased, and the great feudal lords of the region built their aristocratic residences within the city walls (*Osterio Magno* of the Ventimiglia family). Today Cefalù is one of the most renowned tourist resorts in Sicily.

THE CATHEDRAL

Cefalù Cathedral was built by King Roger II of Hauteville to thank Christ the Saviour for having spared his life during a storm at sea. The king also intended the church to be a *Pantheon* for the Hauteville dynasty. The construction was begun in 1131 and went on slowly under Roger's successors, William I and William II, but the original project was never completed. The area of the presbytery is considered to be the oldest, as is confirmed by documents reporting that work on it started on the day of Pentecost 1131. The majestic transept and apse are on a higher level than the front part of the church containing the nave and two aisles. Exquisite Byzantine mosaics decorate the internal walls and the vault of the deep central apse. The figure of Christ Pantocrator in the bowl-shaped vault of the apse, with an expression of mildness on his face, is highly evocative. The façade is framed by two massive bell towers on either side of a triple-arched portico, a later work by Ambrogio da Como (1471). The magnificent entrance portal is decorated with skilfully fashioned marble inlays. The right side of the church is adorned with ogival windows and entwined blind arches. The impressive interior is basilican in plan, with a nave and two aisles divided by 16 columns topped by carved capitals bearing pointed arches. The church contains a fine 12C Romanesque font with four sculpted lions; a great 15C fresco depicting the *Virgin and Child*; two 16C statues of the Annunciation and of an Angel, and a 15C crucifix painted on both sides.

THE MANDRALISCA MUSEUM

The rooms of the museum house the archaeological and artistic collections of Baron *Enrico Piraino di Mandralisca*, including a remarkable collection of archaeological finds from the Greek, Roman and Byzantine ages. The seven rooms display painting and sculpture masterpieces, and pottery from various regions and ages: Aeolian (Bronze Age), geometric (7C BC), Corinthian and Attic (6C-5C BC), as well as terracotta figures and small bronze sculptures dating from the 7C and 4C BC. There is also a vast and remarkable collection of coins from various Greek cities of Sicily, Lipari and *Kephaloidion*. The gallery includes 17C paintings of the Flemish school, a painting by *Franz Van Mieris*, Venetian views from *Guardì*'s school and the famous "Portrait of an Unknown Man" by *Antonello da Messina*. The museum also contains a vast collection of minerals and shells from all over the world.

Himera. Temple of Victory.

HIMERA "The Temple of Victory"

In 648 BC a group of Chalcidians from *Zancle* (Messina), together with inhabitants from *Mylai* (Milazzo) and Syracusan exiles founded the city of Himera, near the river of the same name. Lying on a plateau overlooking the plain which faces the Tyrrhenian Sea, Himera was the westernmost Greek city on the north coast of Sicily. Recent archaeological excavations have brought to light the remains of the city plan with blocks divided by parallel roads. In the surroundings, some necropoli have been explored, as well as a sacred area including three archaic temples. An interesting visit can be made to the *Antiquarium*, where the archaeological finds from the site are collected and exhibited. In the plain to the north of the ancient city, near the old canal harbour, are the remains of the Doric temple known as the "Temple of Victory". This was erected to commemorate the victory of the coalition of Greek Sicilian cities led by Syracuse and Agrigento over the Carthaginians in 480 BC, which marked the first Punic defeat in the Mediterranean. The temple was built in 480-470 BC by craftsmen from Agrigento and Carthaginians taken prisoner during the battle. It is a Doric hexastyle temple with 14 columns on the longer sides, and a cell consisting of prostyle pronaos, naos and opisthodomos. In the ambulatory between the cell walls and the peristasis the floor was paved with limestone slabs, a unique example among Greek temples in Sicily.

SOLÚNTO

According to Thucydides, the city was founded by the Phoenicians, as were Motya and Panormos. The Athenian historian referred to it as *Soloeis*, while Diodorus called the city *Solus*. Cicero wrote of its inhabitants referring to the place-name *Solus-Soluntum*. The Punic name, as appears from coin inscriptions, was *Kfr* (Kafara, i.e. village). Excavations have brought to light the city rebuilt on Mount Catalfano around the mid-4C BC. The older city, mentioned by Thucydides, has not been identified yet, but it probably stood more or less on the same site. The city had always been part of the Carthaginian *epikrateia* until the Roman conquest in 259 BC. At the end of the 2C AD it was voluntarily abandoned by its inhabitants, who probably moved to the site of the earlier settlement. It was completely destroyed by the Saracens and made uninhabitable during their rule of the island. The excavations of *Soluntum*, begun in 1826 and resumed in various periods, show a prevalence of Hellenistic and Roman forms in the city plan, with a geometric Hippodameic layout in which the roads parallel to the main thoroughfare were crossed by steep minor streets, often mere flights of steps. At the entrance to the archaeological site is an *Antiquarium* which houses interesting

sculptural items and illustrates the urban development of the city. From the archaeological site there is a magnificent view of the surroundings – the towns of Santa Flavia, Porticello and Bagheria, the Tyrrhenian Sea as far as the Aeolian islands to the north-east, Termini Imerese with Mount Calogero to the east, and the "Rocca" of Cefalù in the background.

Above: Solúnto. The so-called "Gymnasium", actually a house with a peristyle.

Below: The magnificent panorama from the hill of Solúnto, with a view of the small town of Porticello and, in the background, Mount Calogero.

Top:
Bagheria. Villa Cattolica.

Centre:
Bagheria. Villa Palagonia
(rear part).

Bottom:
Bagheria. Villa Palagonia, one
of the sculpted "Monsters".

BAGHERIA (Villas)

The town first developed around the monumental villas built by the Palermo nobility on the gently-sloping hills of the Palermitan countryside, facing the sea that surrounds Mount Catalfano and the Aspra promontory. In the 17C Prince Giuseppe Branciforte built the first sumptuous residence, *Villa Butera*, and the urban area began to expand along its north-south road axis. Other residences in different styles – from baroque to rococo to neoclassical – were built in the following decades: *La Cattolica*, *Villa Valguarnera* (the most magnificent one, built in 1721 to a plan by Tommaso Maria Napoli), *Villarosa*, built in the late 18C and probably designed by Nicolò Palma, and *Villa Palagonia* (1715), designed by T. M. Napoli, the town's most famous construction because of the bizarre figures of monsters which decorate the entrances and the wall surrounding the property. Of major architectural interest is the scenic front of the building, embellished by a pincer-shaped stairway of remarkable artistic style. Interesting frescoes depicting the "Labours of Hercules" decorate the elliptical vestibule on the first floor. The construction of these majestic villas by Palermitan aristocrats was not strictly linked to the presence of large agricultural estates in the region, although they were all surrounded by gardens (mainly lemon-orchards). The choice of the site had more to do with the emulation of a precise social fashion, that of the "villeggiatura" (summer holiday) as it was conceived in the 18C. The architectural and decorative sumptuousness of these residences still conveys a clear idea of the economic power and lifestyle of the Sicilian aristocracy from the 17C to the beginning of the 19C.

Left: Castle of Carini. Some of its structures.

Bottom: Carini. View of the Castle and town.

CASTLE OF CARINI

The Castle is perched on a rocky outcrop with a splendid view of the town, plain and gulf of Carini, surrounded by a semicircular range of mountains. Its present architectural aspect derives from work carried out between the 12C and 16C. It features an ample internal roofless courtyard with an external stairway leading up to the piano nobile. The Great Hall is covered by an exquisite wooden ceiling, carved and painted according to the late-medieval Sicilian tradition. In the 16C the portals and windows were enlarged and some of the merlons adapted to the introduction of firearms. The piano nobile was renovated between the 18C and 19C, and decorated with wall paintings and several fireplaces. It was in this Castle that the tragedy of the Baroness of Carini took place. On 4 December 1563 Don Cesare Lanza – one of the most powerful aristocrats in the Kingdom – found his beautiful daughter Laura, the wife of Vincenzo La Grua, the Castle owner, in the arms of her lover Ludovico Vernagallo, and killed both of them. Since then, the moving *"Case of the Baroness of Carini"* has been narrated and sung in many versions by storytellers of all times.

PIANA DEGLI ALBANESI
(Byzantine Easter)

From the 15C onwards, Albanian and Greek communities moved to Sicily, fleeing from Turkish and Serbian persecution in their countries of origin. Their descendants, who still live in a few small towns in the province of Palermo, have maintained the original rites of their Greek Orthodox religion. At Piana degli Albanesi, in fact, Easter is celebrated in accordance with the Byzantine rite. The celebrations, known as "The Great Week", differ from those of the Latin rite and begin on the Friday before Palm Sunday,

Women of Piana degli Albanesi in their traditional ceremonial costume (19C engravings by Gaston Vuillier). Some of these costumes – the most ancient ones – are now a valuable family heirloom.

with the commemoration of the resurrection of Lazarus. On Palm Sunday the Bishop of Piana, riding a donkey, leads the procession of believers holding palms in their hands. On the Thursday before Easter, the Bishop performs the Maundy ceremony, and Good Friday ends with the evening procession of believers singing moving funeral songs. On Holy Saturday – at midnight – the churches are closed and all their lights turned out, while people go out in the streets and wait. After several knocks on the church door, the lights are put on, the door is opened, and the priest announces triumphantly "Christ is risen from the dead!". Then everybody lights their candles and enter the church now sparkling with light. On Easter Sunday, after the Mass, hundreds of women parade in the main street wearing the splendid traditional costumes, and the distribution of red-painted eggs takes place near the Church of the Madonna Odighitria.

TRAPANI

The Greeks called the city *Drepanon* (sickle), possibly because of the sickle-shaped stretch of and on which its original nucleus developed, and the name was later maintained by the Romans *Drepanum*). Thanks to its strategic position along the Mediterranean trade routes, in the 8C BC it

became a Phoenician trading centre and later, during the Punic penetration into western Sicily, one of the foremost Carthaginian naval bases together with Lilybaeum, Motya and Panormos. In 260 BC, during the First Punic War, the Carthaginian Hamilcar Barca destroyed Erice, transferred its population to *Drepanon* and fortified the city with new walls and watchtowers. In the summer of 249 BC the Romans were destroyed by Adherbal's Carthaginan fleet in the waters off *Drepanon*. Eight years later, in 241 BC, the Carthaginians were in turn defeated by the fleet of Consul Lutatius Catulus in the decisive naval battle of the Egadi islands, and *Drepanum* passed under Roman rule. In the 9C it was conquered by the Arabs and remained under their rule until 1077. It was then elevated to the rank of a privileged royal city and enjoyed a period of trading and maritime economic prosperity which lasted until the age of Charles V, in the 16C. Although it is the nearest Sicilian port to the North African ports of Barbary (particularly Tunis), Trapani never suffered the direct attacks of pirates. This was due to two facts: the presence of a large Trapanese community in the Tunisian ports (mostly in the Goletta of Tunis), and the strong trading relations between the Jewish merchants of Barbary and those of Trapani (for example in the Giudecca quarter). Nevertheless, over

View of Trapani with the ferry-boats and hydrofoils which link the city to the Egadi islands and North Africa.

the centuries the Crown built adequate defences both in Trapani and the islands in front of its coast, including the Royal Castle and the city walls, the Castle on the Colombaia island, the Ligny Tower, and the Castles on the Egadi islands. Ever since the 8C BC, the sea has been a mainstay of the town's economy. Fishing, the main sector, has always been accompanied by other sea-related activities including coral fishing, salt extraction in the long-established saltpans, and maritime trade. The Pepoli Museum contains a splendid collection of red coral items, testifying to the heights of artistic skill attained by the coral craftsmen.

Trapani. One of the windmills (now restored) which characterize the Trapani seascape.

Opposite page, top: Trapani. The outer harbour and, in the background, the 14C octagonal tower and 15C fortress.

Opposite page, bottom: Trapani. A spectacular view of the salt-pans during salt extraction and piling.

51

SANCTUARY OF THE ANNUNZIATA

Erected between 1315 and 1332, the main body of the Sanctuary was entirely rebuilt in 1760. Of the original structure, the façade with a rose window and the 15C Gothic portal have remained. The fine baroque bell tower, with pilaster strips and half-columns, dates from 1650. The single-nave interior was reconstructed in the 18C by Giovanni B. Amico and contains remarkable works of art: a *Virgin and Child* by Nino Pisano, known as the "Madonna di Trapani"; the *Fishermen's Chapel*, used as a baptistery since 1468, featuring a groin vault frescoed in the 16C with a story from Genesis; the 16C *Sailors' Chapel*, in Renaissance style with Gothic reminiscences. In the Sanctuary, or *Virgin's Chapel*, there is a magnificent marble arch with relief figures of the Prophets and of the Eternal Father by Antonio and Giacomo Gagini, with a bronze gate executed by Giuliano Musarra in 1591. On the polychrome marble altar of St Albert's Chapel is the silver statue of the Saint by Vincenzo Bonaiuto.

PALAZZO DELLA GIUDECCA

Situated in the old city centre, in via della Giudecca, the heart of the old Jewish quarter, this splendid building is in a composite architectural style which makes it particularly interesting. The façade features an ogival portal with a richly ornate frame. The rectangular windows also have elaborate frames. The building is flanked by a tower which, in the upper part, is entirely covered by diamond-pointed ashlars, a typical feature of the Italian Renaissance style. The corbels on the top of the building formerly supported a battlemented parapet (now lost) for defensive purposes.

Above: Trapani.
Pepoli Museum. "Madonna and Child with Saints" (early 15C), by the Master of the Polyptych of Trapani.

THE PEPOLI MUSEUM

The *Pepoli Regional Museum* displays interesting collections of archaeological finds, paintings, sculptures and other artistic items. There is a notable collection of items by *Trapanese coral craftsmen*, masters of an art which has developed here since the second half of the 16C. Today a new school, following in the footsteps of the ancient tradition, is giving fresh impetus to this precious and creative handicraft activity. The "*Strada del Sale*" (Salt Road) offers another interesting itinerary through the salt-pans and pools all along the coast between Trapani and Marsala, ending with a visit to the "*Museo del Sale*" (Salt Museum) at Nubia.

Opposite page, left:
Trapani. Sanctuary of the Annunziata.
Opposite page, right:
Trapani. Palazzo della Giudecca and the tower with "diamond-pointed" ashlars.

Above: Erice. The Torretta, built by Count Agostino Pepoli.

Top, right: Erice. The Norman castle, known as "Castello di Venere" (Castle of Venus).

Bottom: Erice. The Church of the Assunta and its massive bell tower, 26 m high.

ERICE

A naturally fortified Elymian city perched on the top of the huge promontory overlooking Trapani, Erice was the site of one of the most famous pagan sanctuaries of antiquity, dedicated to the goddess of fertility called Astarte by the Phoenicians, Aphrodite by the Greeks, and Venus Erycina by the Romans. The goddess was the protector of sailors and was venerated by all Mediterranean peoples, so the sacred site was regularly frequented by pilgrims and believers. A Carthaginian stronghold, the city was stormed by Pyrrhus in 277 BC and reconquered by the Carthaginians in 275 BC. During the First Punic War, in 260 BC, it was destroyed by the Carthaginian army and its population was deported to Drepano, present-day Trapani. In Roman times the sanctuary became the head of a religious confederation including 17 Sicilian cities, and was protected by a Roman garrison. Under Tiberius the whole sacred area was restored, thus maintaining its original religious importance. No historical information of note exists on Byzantine Erice. The town was still inhabited and farms were scattered over its fertile surroundings. Around 831 AD the stronghold was occupied by the Arabs and called Gebel-Hamed. During the Kingdom of Sicily, in the 12C, its name was changed to Monte San Giuliano, and a period of great prosperity began. The town was repopulated and underwent extensive architectural transformation which gave it its present-day unique appearance. The urban layout is particularly interesting. The boundary walls, bearing traces of different ages, enclose a network of small streets leading to medieval houses with picturesque small courtyards embellished by stairways and loggias full of flowers. Among the most notable medieval buildings are the Church of the Assunta (1314), the main church, with its massive bell tower (originally a watchtower), and the "Castle of Venus", erected in the Middle Ages, perhaps on the site of the ancient sanctuary of Venus Erycina, together with the Balio and Pepoli Castles. A walk through the little streets of the town may be an extremely evocative experience, especially if low clouds cover the top of Mount San Giuliano, creating a soft haze and a muffled, fairy-tale atmosphere. Erice is the seat of a scientific institution of great

international prestige, the "Centro Ettore Majorana", where conferences of scientists from all over the world are periodically held to discuss scientific issues in all fields and their repercussions on the world's society.

ERICE – The Main Church (Assunta)

The church was built in 1314 by King Frederick III of Aragon. The façade has retained its original medieval style, while the portico with pointed arches dates from the 15C. The detached bell tower was originally a watchtower. The interior was completely transformed by the lengthy and complex renovation work started in 1865, so that only the two-aisle plan and the two rows of columns bearing pointed arches remain of the original 14C structure. The side chapels feature two statues of the *Madonna and Child* (one from *Laurana*'s school) and a *Madonna* attributed to F. Laurana, perhaps the work of Domenico Gagini. An imposing marble statue sculpted in 1523 by Giuliano Mancino stands in the presbytery. The Crucifix chapel features a 15C star-shaped vault.

Above: Erice. A typical courtyard with flowers.

Below: View of the vast plain below Erice.

Above: Scopello.
The beautiful small cove with
the 16C tunny-fishery.

SCOPELLO

An old agricultural village, Scopello stretches to the sides of an 18C *baglio* (here, a sort of large manor house with buildings opening onto a central courtyard) built on the site of a pre-existing medieval hamlet. The nearby beautiful small cove houses the 16C buildings of the "tonnara" (tunny-fishery), which was established at the beginning of the 17C and remained active until a few years ago. The charm of its rocky coastline and the beauty of the landscape make it one of the most emblematic and fascinating places in the island. Within a short distance, on the slopes of Mount Speziale, in the coastal area between Scopello and San Vito Lo Capo, is the "Zingaro Regional Natural Reserve". This is an untouched oasis of Mediterranean vegetation, with carrob trees, impressive dwarf palms, wild olives, the typical Mediterranean maquis with brooms, asphodels, euphorbias and, in the early Sicilian spring, luxuriant irises, gillyflowers, daffodils and calendulas. Looking west, towards San Vito Lo Capo, a foot-path on the slopes of the mountains winds its way across the natural reserve, in a beautiful coastal landscape guarded over by 16C watch-towers.

CASTELLAMMARE DEL GOLFO

In pre-Hellenic times, the town on the gulf was used as a landing place and trading centre by the Elymian populations of Erice and Segesta. In the early Middle Ages it was fortified in order to protect the port, where wheat and other agricultural products were loaded. Work was be-

*Above: Calatafimi.
Ossuary Monument at
"Pianto Romano". The bronze
bas-reliefs depict scenes
from Garibaldi's expedition
of 1860.*

gun to transform the original medieval castle into a tunny-fishery. In the 14C it was isolated by the cutting of an isthmus. After the construction of a new outer breakwater, the port continued to handle trade, and to be a harbour for fishing and pleasure boats. In the old town centre, facing via Garibaldi, is the Main Church, built in the 17C and altered several times in the course of the following centuries. In via Ponte Castello is the small Church of the Rosario, with a richly ornate 16C portal. Further on is the *Castle*, to the right of the port with the quay where small fishing boats are moored.

CALATAFIMI – Ossuary Monument at "Pianto Romano"
"HERE WE MAKE ITALY OR DIE"

This is what Garibaldi was reported to have said to Nino Bixio and to his troops on the day of the historic battle against the Bourbon army led by General Landi (15 May 1860).

On 11 May Garibaldi and his "Mille" (Thousand men), supported by numerous Sicilian "picciotti" (brave fighting lads), landed at Marsala where, in the name of Italy and of Victor Emmanuel II of Savoy, he started the successful expedition which was to lead to the liberation of the whole of the south of Italy. On 15 May, at dawn, Garibaldi's troops arrived at Calatafimi, garrisoned by Bourbon troops. The battle broke out violently at noon and went on throughout the afternoon until, at dusk, a decisive attack by Garibaldi's troops put the enemy to flight. On 13 May, at Salemi, Garibaldi had become dictator of Sicily in the name of Victor Emmanuel II. Triumphantly welcomed by the population, he continued the fight against the Bourbon army and, on 30 May, conquered Salemi thanks to the support given by the Sicilian people.

The ossuary monument (1892) is the work of the architect Ernesto Basile. The bronze bas-reliefs depict scenes from the expedition: the landing at Marsala and two episodes of the battle at Calatafimi.

*Opposite page, bottom:
Castellammare del Golfo.*

Above: Segesta. The solitary and noble Temple, steeped in the beauty of a truly unique landscape.

SEGESTA (Egesta)

The city of Egesta was historically important because of its perpetual rivalry with nearby Selinunte for control over the fertile lands crossed by the Mazaro River. The earliest armed conflicts date back to 580-576 BC. In 415 BC Segesta called for help from Athens against Selinunte and Syracuse. After this disastrous expedition it entered into an alliance with the Carthaginians which resulted in the destruction of Selinunte in 409 BC and subsequently of Himera, Agrigento and Gela. In 397 BC Segesta, a Punic allied city, was besieged by the Syracusans and, after changing fortunes, at the end of the 4C BC it was conquered and destroyed by Agathocles, a tyrant of Syracuse, who named it Dikaepolis.

In 267 BC it joined forces with Pyrrhus, king of Epyrus, during his successful two-year campaign in Sicily. At the beginning of the First Punic War it was one of the first Sicilian cities to pass over to the Romans. For this reason it was always respected by Rome and became *libera et immunis*, a free and immune city. It was assigned vast territories and, as its large estates employed a great number of servants, it was a starting point for the slaves' revolt of 104 BC.

THE TEMPLE OF SEGESTA

This imposing construction stands solitary and solemn in the middle of a deserted landscape. Probably built in the last thirty years of the 5C BC outside the double stretch of city walls, the temple is considered one of the most important examples of Doric style. It stands on a stepped base, covering an upper surface area of 61.15 x 26.25 m, over which is a peristyle with 36 unfluted columns, 6 on the fronts and 14 along the sides, still bearing the entablature and tympanums. The columns, consisting of 10-12 drums, are 9.36 m high (including the capitals) with a diameter of 1.95 m (base) and 1.56 m (top) and intercolumns of 2.40 m. Since the building is roofless, many scholars have suggested that its construction was interrupted in 409 BC. Others, instead, believe that the roof was not built for the specific purpose of using the temple as an open-air enclosure devoted to Elymian rites. It seems likely that, during one of the rare periods of reduced political and military tension between Segesta and Selinunte, the Segestans turned to the renowned workmanship of architects from Selinunte to give their main

Below: Segesta. The Theatre, overlooking the valley.

sacred building the monumental appearance of a Greek temple.

THE THEATRE OF SEGESTA

The theatre stands on the southern slopes of Mount Barbaro, on the site of the North Acropolis of the city. Excavations carried out in 1927 brought to light prehistoric material and remains of buildings dating from the 10C-9C BC, probably used for religious purposes, in a cave beneath the cavea. The theatre is believed to date from the mid-3C BC. However, the actual chronology of its construction is controversial. It was probably built in the 2C BC and altered and restored in the Augustan age. The wide semicircular cavea, 63 m in diameter, is divided into seven wedges with twenty tiers of seats hewn out of the rock and others supported by limestone blocks. The stage is separated from the cavea by open passageways and features square parascenia decorated with two figures of the Greek divinity Pan. The theatre, which has undergone reconstruction and restoration work, is now used for classical drama performances every two years, thus becoming "the millenary scene for the world's classics", theatrical productions which conjure

Above: Segesta. Temple.

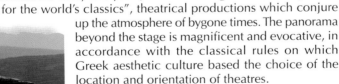

up the atmosphere of bygone times. The panorama beyond the stage is magnificent and evocative, in accordance with the classical rules on which Greek aesthetic culture based the choice of the location and orientation of theatres.

Above: Favignana. The "Mattanza" (ritual tunny killing).

Below: Favignana. One of the numerous open-cast tufa quarries.

EGADI ISLANDS

The Egadi islands, the ancient *Aegates*, are **Favignana**, the main island and administrative centre, **Levanzo**, **Marettimo** and the islets of **Formica** and **Maraone**. Situated within a short distance from Trapani, they have been inhabited since prehistoric times (Upper Paleolithic). Evidence of a Phoenician-Punic settlement has been found on Favignana (the ancient *Aegusa*). A Carthaginian naval base during the Punic Wars, the island was occupied by the Romans in 241 BC following the victory of Consul Lutatius Catulus over the Carthaginian fleet in its waters. In the late Middle Ages the Santa Caterina and the San Giacomo forts were built to defend the island. Favignana is the seat of the most important tunny-fishery in Sicily, where the traditional *mattanza* (ritual tunny killing) takes place every year. Inside the "Grotta del Genovese" (Genoese cave) on Levanzo (the ancient *Phorbantia*) rock drawings and paintings have been discovered which seem to indicate the presence of cultural *facies* from different ages (Paleolithic-Mesolithic). Two series of drawings decorate the walls of the cave, one with animal figures (cattle, horses, deer), the other with human figures hunting or dancing and idols suggesting the performance of propitiatory rites. A pleasant boat trip can be taken along the steep coasts of the island, which are scattered with caves opening out onto the sea and dominated by the Faraglione, a cone-shaped rock connected to the land by a short isthmus. Marettimo, formerly called *Hiera* or *Hieromesus*, is mostly steeply sloping except for a short stretch of coast along which the urban area extends with its small harbour. With its springs and clear and unspoilt sea swarming with fish, it is the most fascinating of the Egadi islands.

The Stagnone lagoon.
In the foreground, the
geometrically arranged
salt-pans. In the centre, the
island which is the site of the
ancient Phoenician-Punic city
of Motya.

Below: Motya. Whitaker
Museum. Marble statue
of a "Youth" (second quarter
of the 5C BC).

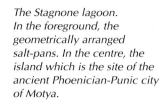

MOTYA

The *Stagnone* lagoon is one of the most fascinating landscapes in Sicily. Several islets covered with the typical Mediterranean scrub vegetation enclose a vast stretch of water, protected from the open sea by the low contours of Isola Lunga. A natural haven for sailors, with waters swarming with fish, in the 8C BC it must have appeared to the Phoenicians as the ideal place to establish the first base of their trading empire in the western Mediterranean. As the power of Carthage grew, Motya became the main Punic military base, continuously at war with the Greek cities of Sicily. In 397 BC it was conquered and destroyed by Dionysius I of Syracuse. It was reconquered by the Carthaginians the following year, and a new community was founded at Lilybaeum. This event adversely affected Motya's destiny, as the city, even though it was inhabited until the 3C BC, never recovered and eventually vanished from history. The entire island is covered with the remains of the ancient city, surrounded by a long stretch of walls with watchtowers, two main gates and several smaller ones scattered along a perimeter of about 3 km. The north gate opens onto a road which used to join the island to Birgi, on the mainland. In ancient times the road, now submerged, was 1 m above the Stagnone waters. It is interesting to visit the *archaic necropolis* (late 8C-6C BC), consisting of cinerary tombs cut into the rock. Not far away is the *tophet*, a Phoenician sanctuary where first-born children were sacrificed to Baal Hammon. The discovery of ancient Motya was made possible by the enthusiastic work of the English merchant Giuseppe Whitaker, the owner of the island, who directed the first successful excavations during the last century. Motya's Museum displays the archaeological material found on the island, in the Birgi necropolis and in ancient Lilybaeum. The most interesting item is a beautiful *marble statue* found on Motya in 1979, portraying a young man dressed in a long pleated tunic enhancing his strong athletic figure, the work of a Greek artist from the 5C BC.

Top: Marsala. Aerial view of the present-day town with its spacious harbour which handles cargo ships of over 5,000 tons used for wine exportation.

Centre: Marsala. The Duomo (1628), dedicated to St Thomas of Canterbury.

Below: Marsala. Marble bust of Giuseppe Garibaldi, the "Hero of the two Worlds".

MARSALA

The Punic name Lilybaeum, from Capo Boeo, was changed by the Arabs to *Marsa-Alì* or Allah, hence Marsala. According to ancient sources, the origins of the city are linked to the destruction of Motya (a Phoenician city founded in the 8C BC) by Dionysius I, a tyrant of Syracuse, in 397 BC. Refugees from Motya fled to Capo Boeo and, perhaps together with native populations, founded the city of Lilybaeum. In 350 BC the city was fortified with massive walls and became one of the Carthaginian strongholds in Sicily. Conquered by the Romans in 241 BC, it maintained its military and commercial power in the central Mediterranean and became the seat of the Quaestor for the western provinces. Under the Arabs, who conquered it in 830 AD, the city continued to flourish as a hub of trade with Africa. The Normans occupied Marsala in 1072. Between the 12C and 14C, the medieval urban layout was developed with the construction of religious buildings and monasteries. The town took on its present Renaissance-baroque aspect between the 17C and 18C, when the main civil and religious buildings were erected or reconstructed and surrounded by a circle of bastions with four monumental gateways. Today the town's economy is mostly based on the wine industry, particularly on the production of the famous Marsala wine, introduced by the Englishman G. Woodhouse in 1773 and continued by the Ingham and Florio families with the establishment of new and modern wineries throughout the region.

SELINUNTE

The monumental ruins of the ancient Greek city of Selinunte stretch over the plateau and the gentle hills facing the "African" sea. The date of Selinunte's foundation is controversial. According to Diodorus, the city was founded between 651 and 650 BC, while according to Thucydides its foundation dates back to 629-628 BC. The first urban nucleus was established on the steep-sided plateau (about 50 m above sea level) situated between the valley of the Modione River (the ancient *Selinos*) to the west and the "Gorgo di Cottone" valley to the east. This was the Acropolis. Behind it, to the north, were the city's residential quarters. The name of the city probably derived from the river which flowed to the west of its boundaries, the *Selinos*, or, as others have suggested, from a wild plant, a sort of celery ("selinon") which grows locally and whose leaves were depicted in the early coins minted at Selinunte. The westernmost Greek outpost, the city extended its influence over the fertile coastal plains, from the mouth of the Platani River to the east, to the mouth of the *Mazarus* River to the west, and as far as present-day Poggioreale to the north. The Selinuntines had to fight fierce battles against a coalition of Elymian cities. These were followed by a long period of peaceful relations with its neighbours, which was accompanied by the urban and architectural development of the city. As Diodorus wrote in his *Histories*, Selinunte was the only Greek colony to be aligned with Carthage during the first Punic invasion of Sicily in 480 BC, but it was not subjected to retaliation by the Greeks (Syracusans and Agrigentines) who led the successful coalition. After the defeat at Himera, Selinunte changed its policy and allied with Syracuse, until the powerful Carthaginian army, eager for revenge, besieged, conquered and destroyed it in 409 BC. It was, however, dur-

Selinunte. A suggestive night view of Temple E, probably dedicated to Hera, the Roman Juno, as is suggested by a votive stele with a dedicatory inscription to the goddess found in the temple.

Above: Demeter Malophoros Sanctuary.

ing the First Punic War that Selinunte's power and prestige were finally given the *coup de grâce*. In order to prevent it from falling into Roman hands, the Carthaginians dismantled all the residual fortifications and destroyed the urban areas, transferring the population to Lilybaeum.

THE DEMETER MALOPHOROS SANCTUARY

The *Malophoros* sacred area, situated to the west of the Modione River (the ancient *Selinos*), is entered through a propylaeum at the end of a sacred path. The temple is in the style of the earliest temples, recalling the pre-Doric *megara*. On the same site are also other sacred enclosures, one dedicated to *Zeus Melichios* and one dedicated to Pasicratea, the name given by the Selinuntines to Persephone or Kore, the daughter of Demeter and wife of Pluto, the queen of the Underworld and of the dead. Another enclosure to the left of the propylaeum was dedicated to *Hecate* or *Artemis triform*, a three-faced deity – at the same time *Hecate, Artemis* and *Proserpina* – represented by a single body with the heads of a lion, a horse and a she-wolf. Outside the *Malophoros* enclosure, archaeological excavations have brought to light a construction dating from the mid-6C BC, referred to as *Temple M*, measuring 20.40 x 10.85 m and recently identified as a monumental fountain with access from a flight of steps.

THE ROCCA DI CUSA QUARRIES

The modelled limestone blocks are scattered all over the ground, as if they had just been extracted from the rock. The landscape is characterized by the rural environment typical of this part of Sicily, covered with a rich vegetation as it certainly must have been 2300 years ago, when Selinuntine quarrymen extracted the cylindrical blocks used to make columns for their temples. Looking around, it seems as if the quarrymen's work should be resumed before long. But this is not the case. The scene is that of 409 BC, the very day when the terrible historic events began which would eventually lead to the annihilation of their city. The work of the skilful Selinuntine masters has stopped for ever, never to be resumed again.

Above:
Rocca di Cusa quarries.

Below: Selinunte.
Temples in the Acropolis.

Agrigento. Valley of the Temples. The so-called Temple of the Dioscuri. The name derives from the Greek "Dios kuroi", i.e. "Sons of Zeus", the twins Castor and Pollux. According to Spartan primitive mythology, the twins were born, together with Helen and Clytemnestra, from the egg conceived by Leda with Zeus, who appeared to her in the form of a swan.

Opposite page, smaller photo: The Temple of Heracles.

Below: Agrigento. Regional Archaeological Museum. Marble torso of a "Greek warrior" (480-470 BC), whose fragments were brought to light in the area of the Temple of Zeus in 1940.

AGRIGENTO

The Agrigento area has been inhabited since prehistoric times, as is testified by archaeological finds dating from the Copper and Bronze Ages. The Aeneolithic settlement of *Serraferlicchio* gave its name to an indigenous "*facies*" of prehistoric Sicily after a large quantity of skilfully worked pottery with black decorations on a red background was discovered there. The earliest traces of Greek presence date back to the end of the 7C BC and include the *archaic necropolis of Montelusa*, situated on the coast to the west of present-day San Leone. The founding of Akragas in 580 BC marked an important step in the plans of the Rhodian-Cretans from Gela to expand their political and military influence towards the western coasts and the interior. The ancient history of the city is mainly linked to the figure of Phalaris, described as a cruel tyrant, who was, however, responsible for its rapid urban development. This early nucleus, protected to the north by the hill which constituted the Acropolis – the *Rupe Atenea* – extended as far as the valley characterized by the low ridge where the monumental Doric temples were built. During Phalaris' rule, from 570 to 555 BC, Akragas grew more powerful and extended its possessions to the detriment of the Sicans, who were driven back towards the interior or subdued. This expansionist policy was continued by Phalaris' successor, the tyrant Theron (488-472 BC), who brought the city to the height of its splendour. After the victory over the Carthaginians at Himera in 480 BC, he extended the city boundaries as far as the Tyrrhenian coasts and the coastline between the mouth of the Salso River (the southern course of the Himera) and that of the Halikos (the present-day Platani River) to the south. This first armed clash was followed by a prosperous and active period marked by the construction of temples, public and private buildings and fortifications. At that time, Agrigento probably had the highest standard of living of all the Greek cities of Sicily, as reported by Empedocles, a physician, philosopher and orator, the city's most distinguished citizen of all time, who was also renowned in Greece, and who thus defined his fellow citizens: *"The people of Agrigento enjoy the pleasures and luxuries of the world as if they were to die the next day, but make their buildings as if they were to live forever"*. And that must have been true, so much so that a contemporary of Empedocles', a physician from Agrigento named Acron, felt the need to exhort his fellow citizens to moderation in a book entitled "The Diet of the Healthy People". Pindar, the Greek lyric poet who lived between 518 and 438 BC, thus sang the praises of Agrigento: *"...Thee I invoke, city of Persephone, the most beautiful city of mortal men, lover of splendour rising by Akragas over the towered hill..."* (Pindar, 12th *Pythian Ode*). Apart from luxury and opulence, Theron's court promoted

*Agrigento.
Valley of the Temples.
The majestic remains of the
temple dedicated to
Olympian Zeus. Steps lead up
to the sacrificial altar, which
preceded the east front of the
imposing Olympieion.*

*Agrigento.
Valley of the Temples.
A gigantic "Telamon".*

poetry and the arts, and attracted scientists, philosophers, sculptors and painters such as Pythagoras, Myron, Simonides and Zeuxis. The people of Agrigento normally practised sports, particularly equestrian sports, and there were horsemen and charioteers among them who had scored more than one victory at Olympia. Towards the mid-5C BC a democratic regime was established and the city enjoyed a period of relative peace until the Carthaginian invasion of Sicily. In 406 BC Agrigento was besieged and burnt down by the Carthaginian general Himilco, and its population sought refuge in Leontinoi, under the protection of Syracuse. Under Timoleon, who defeated the Carthaginians (c 340 BC) and is considered Agrigento's second founder, the city rose again from its ruins and was given a new urban layout, as is witnessed by the ruins of the Hellenistic-Roman quarter.

THE VALLEY OF THE TEMPLES

On a ridge in the valley at the foot of the hill which is the site of present-day Agrigento are the prestigious remains of the ancient city. This is one of the largest archaeological sites in the Mediterranean area. Temples, public buildings, theatres, and whole quarters stand out against superb natural scenery with the sparkling "African" sea in the background. Because of the large number of sanctuaries dedicated to divinities of the ancient world, this enchanted site has well deserved the name of "Valley of the Temples". On the edge of the Valley are the majestic remains of the temples of Hercules, Hera Lacinia (Juno) and the Temple of Concord. Within the boundaries of what is thought to be the Agora, the Sanctuary of Esculapius (Asclepeion), the Olympieion and the Sanctuary of the Chthonic Deities (Temple of the Dioscuri;

Temple "L"; Temple "I") have been identified. On the Acropolis is a Temple, probably dedicated to Athena and later adapted to the Christian cult (Church of Santa Maria dei Greci). Outside the ancient urban nucleus is the Temple of Demeter, also transformed into the Christian Church of San Biagio. Near the Archaeological Museum is the so-called *Oratory of Phalaris*, actually a small Roman temple.

THE TEMPLE OF HERACLES (Hercules)

The ruins of the *Temple of Heracles* stand in a superb position on the lower spurs of the *Hill of the Temples*, on the site where the Byzantines cut their way through the hillside through Gate IV, leading to the road running from the Emporium (the port of San Leone) to the Valley of the Temples. An analysis of the remains has shown that this is the oldest of the *Sanctuaries of Agrigento*, probably erected towards the end of the 6C BC. It is a peripteral hexastyle temple, 37 m long, with a peristasis of 38 columns, 6 on the fronts and 15 on the sides. Together with the bronze statue of the demigod, the interior housed a painting by the famous Greek artist *Zeuxis*, which depicted Hercules as a child in his cradle and his mother Alcmena helping him to strangle the snakes sent by Hera to kill him.

Based on a very ingenious and innovative design, the majestic **OLYMPIEION** was built after the victory of Syracuse and Agrigento over the Carthaginians at Himera in 480 BC. Punic prisoners taken during the battle were employed in its construction, and it was still unfinished when the city was conquered and burnt during the Carthaginian retaliatory attack in 406 BC. With its majestic proportions it is considered to be the largest temple in the western world together with *Temple G* at Selinunte. On the rectangular base (56.30 x 113.45 m) are five steps leading to the limiting ambulatories. It was a pseudo-peripteral temple, enclosed by a wall out of which projected 7 x 14 half-columns, each corresponding to an internal pillar. In the middle of the wide intercolumns, at about 13 m from the stylobate, were the plastic figures of gigantic *telamones* which decorated the exterior and, together with the pillars, contributed to support the heavy entablature.

Agrigento. Valley of the Temples. Temple of Concord. This is one of the best preserved Doric temples of the ancient Greek world. Its perfect state of conservation is due to the fact that it continued to be used over the centuries. Situated in the middle of the Hill of the Temples, it dominates the surrounding valleys with its elegant and perfect proportions.

*Agrigento.
Valley of the Temples.
Temple of Hera Lacinia.
Burnt by the Carthaginians
in 406 BC, it was restored
by the Romans.*

THE TEMPLE OF HERA LACINIA (Juno)

This temple stands on the highest point of the *Hill of the Temples*, on a superbly panoramic site. Built in the purest Doric style on a four-stepped stylobate, it measures 38.15 x 16.90 m, with 34 columns, 6 on the fronts and 13 on the sides. It is a peripteral hexastyle temple with an in-antis cella (28.68 x 9.93 m). Part of the enclosing walls and several drums of the columns of the opisthodomos and pronaos are still extant. The temple was built shortly before the Temple of Concord, dating from the 5C BC, and the two buildings have similar architectural features. Burnt down by the Carthaginians in 406 BC, it was restored by the Romans. Near the east front is a large *sacrificial altar* (29.80 x 7.25 m).

THE TEMPLE OF CONCORD

Together with the *Temple of Hera* and *Paestum* (*Posidonion*) and the Athenian *Theseion*, this is one of the best-preserved Doric temples of the ancient Greek world. Its perfect state of conservation is due to the fact that it continued to be used over the centuries. In 597 AD it was transformed into a Christian basilica and consecrated by the bishop of Agrigento, Gregory. A peripteral hexastyle temple with 6 x 13 columns, it stands in the middle of the Hill of the Temples, dominating with its elegant proportions the valleys of the ancient urban centre to the north and the valley sloping towards the "African" sea to the south, as the Latin poet Virgil saw and described it in the Aeneid.

*Opposite page:
Agrigento. Regional
Archaeological Museum.
Marble statue of a "Youth",
a Greek original dating
from the early 5C BC.*

THE REGIONAL ARCHAEOLOGICAL MUSEUM

The museum is one of the masterpieces of Franco Minissi, the architect who devoted his life and professional activity to modernizing the design of archaeological museums in Italy and abroad (among his works are the famous Etruscan Museum of Villa Giulia in Rome and the Solar Barque Museum in Cairo). Together with its counterpart in Syracuse, the Agrigento Museum is one of the greatest cultural achievements of the Sicilian Region – indeed one of the foremost archaeological museums in Sicily – and is visited by crowds of tourists every year. It was set up in the monumental area of the *bouleterion* and *ekklesiasterion*, on the hillock of San Nicola, and incorporates part of the convent adjoining the church of the same name. The material is arranged chronologically and divided into two main sectors, one concerning Agrigento and its history, and the other concerning a part of the archaeological sites of the provinces of Caltanissetta and Gela, which have their own museums. Room 1 houses maps and plans of Agrigento and the Museum plan. *Room 2* displays prehistoric and protohistoric material dating from the 2nd and 1st millennia BC and relating to the native populations and the area where the Greek Akragas was founded by the Rhodian-Cretans in 580 BC. It includes items from the necropoli, chronologically arranged in showcases; early and medium Bronze Age pottery from the *Aeneolithic culture of Serraferlicchio* (from Cannatello and Monserrato), and early Iron Age material from the *culture of Sant'Angelo Muxaro*. *Room 3* displays the collection of vases from the civic museum and the Giudice collection, including items from the most recent excavations. The strictly chronological itinerary includes *red-figured and black-figured Attic vases* dating from the 6C and 5C BC and Graeco-Italiot production from the 5C to the 3C BC. The 19 rooms of the museum preserve the priceless historical and artistic vestiges of the Greek Akragas and of the area under its dominion.

Agrigento. Regional Archaeological Museum. Above: Head of a kouros or sphinx (550-530 BC).

Below: Agrigento. Regional Archaeological Museum. Red-figured Attic vase (5C BC) depicting "Apollo's Procession".

Luigi Pirandello in Agrigento.

Below: Agrigento. The solitary pine with the limestone block where Luigi Pirandello's ashes are kept.

LUIGI PIRANDELLO

Luigi Pirandello was born in Agrigento in 1867, of a wealthy bourgeois family. His interest in philology led him to attend university first in Palermo, then in Rome and finally in Bonn, where he took his degree in 1891 with a dissertation on Greek-Sicilian dialects and worked one year as a language teacher of Italian. On his return to Italy, he joined the Roman literary milieu, collaborating in the *Nuova Antologia* with poems and critical essays. After he and his wife Antonietta Portulano (who bore him three children) fell into financial trouble, Pirandello began teaching stylistics and literature at the Normal College for Women in Rome (1897-1922). After World War I he wrote most of the plays which were to make him famous throughout the world. From 1926 to 1936 he directed a theatrical company whose star performer was Marta Abba, an actress to whom he dedicated his plays "Vestire gli ignudi" (To clothe the naked) and "L'amica delle mogli" (The wives' friend). A member of the "Accademia d'Italia" from 1929 and winner of the Nobel Prize for Literature in 1934, he died in Rome in 1936, while working on his drama "I giganti della montagna" (The giants of the mountain). His vast production of novels, plays and essays places him among the foremost Italian and European authors of the early 20C.

PELAGIE ISLANDS

The archipelago of the Pelagie consists of the islands of Lampedusa and Linosa and the islet of Lampione. Lampedusa, the largest and most important of the three, with a coastal perimeter of 33.3 km, is 205 km from Marina di Palma in Sicily, 113 km from the coast of Tunisia and 150 km from Malta. Its natural harbour is made up of three bays: Cala Salina, Cala Guitgia and Cala Palme. With its sheer coastline interrupted here and there by a few solitary beaches, the island is an ideal destination for "alternative" holidays. The numerous caves along the coast were once inhabited by seals. The vegetation abounds with prickly pears, fig trees, oleanders and carrob trees. Fishing, especially for sardines and anchovies, is widely practised. Linosa, 42 km from Lampedusa, is of volcanic origin. The islet of Lampione is uninhabited. The islands were part of the Kingdom of Sicily in the Middle Ages, but the frequent raids by North African pirates caused a gradual decline in population. Only in 1843 did the Bourbon king Ferdinand II repopulate them. Today the Pelagie are linked by regular services to Sicily, particularly to Trapani, and attract a large number of "connoisseur" tourists every year.

Above: Lampedusa.

Below: A suggestive sunset on Lampedusa.

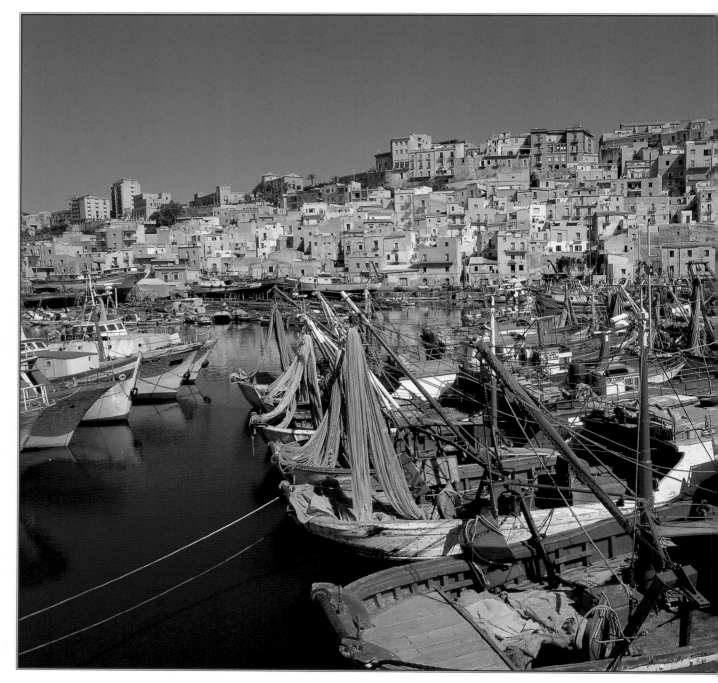

Sciacca. The port.

SCIACCA (Monte Kronio)

Identified as the ancient *Termae Selinuntinae*, the modern town lies on a long terraced hillside area dominating the wide fishing port. With its abundant thermal waters on the slopes of Mount San Calogero, a 360 m high calcareous mountain overlooking the urban centre, Sciacca is the main spa town of Sicily. It has been known since ancient times for the therapeutic properties of its waters and natural "stufe vaporose", caves full of hot dense stream coming out of the karst cavities on the top of the mountain. According to Diodorus, the first to exploit the town's hydrothermal basin was Daedalus. The territory has been inhabited since the Neolithic and Aeneolithic Ages (5000-3000 BC), as is witnessed by the important prehistoric remains found in the caves. The old town centre offers an interesting itinerary including monuments ranging from the Middle Ages to the 17C and the baroque 18C.

HERACLEA MINOA

Situated on a plateau sloping down to the sea near the mouth of the Platani River, the city was founded by the Selinuntines in the 6C BC, on the site of a supposed Mycenaean settlement. It was named Heraclea by the Spartan Euryleon, the head of a group of new colonists who settled in the city after taking part in Dorieus' unsuccessful campaign in Sicily. The name Minoa is related to Minos, the legendary Cretan king who, having come to Sicily on an expedition, was killed in the royal palace of the Sican king Kokalos. The foundation of Minoa by the Selinuntines formed part of their plans to expand their territories eastwards, in competition with Agrigento. In the early 5C BC, the city passed to Theron, a tyrant of Agrigento (488-472 BC) who, having identified the site of Minos' tomb, returned his bones to the Cretans, as reported by the Greek Sicilian historian Diodorus in the fourth book of his *Histories*. Involved in the Greek-Carthaginian wars, the city was destroyed and sacked. Under the Romans it became a *civitas decumana*, as Cicero reported in his *Verrines*. It was abandoned at the end of the 1C BC and eventually disappeared from history.

Heraclea Minoa.

Caltanissetta. View of the modern town with the expanding post-war urban quarters.

CALTANISSETTA

The earliest historical data on Caltanissetta go back to the Middle Ages, when Count Roger of Hauteville occupied the territory and took the Petrarossa Castle, probably an Arab stronghold, in 1086. The first urban nucleus thus developed around the Norman Priory of St John. It is very interesting to visit the city's Archaeological Museum, which houses a notable collection of archaeological material discovered during excavations on the outskirts of the town (Mount San Giuliano) and in the archaeological sites of Capodarso, Sabucina and Gibil Gabib (a vast necropolis with prehistoric and Greek rock-cut tombs).

Gibil Gabib: An indigenous centre, it was Hellenized first by Gela and then by Agrigento in the late 6C-5C BC, during its territorial expansion over the valleys of the Himera River (now the Salso) as far as the Tyrrhenian coasts. Sections of the fortified walls are still extant. The mountain was abandoned in the 4C BC.

Sabucina: A Sicel indigenous centre with remains of circular huts and rock-cut chamber tombs from the early to the late Bronze Age (12C-9C BC, Pantalica culture). As in the cases of the other indigenous centres in the Himera valley, in the course of the 6C BC it was occupied first by Gela and then by Agrigento, and thus Hellenized. It was abandoned at the end of the 4C BC.

Capodarso: An indigenous centre situated 795 m above sea level on a plateau dominating the Salso valley. On the basis of archaeological research, it has been classified as belonging to the Sant'Angelo Muxaro-Polizzello cultural "facies". Hellenized during the 4C BC it was abandoned in the early 3C BC. The necropolis has been explored and a section of the defensive works has been brought to light.

GELA

Founded in 689 BC by the Rhodians of Antiphemus and the Cretans of Entimus, it took its name from the nearby *Gela* River. The first tyrant of Gela was Cleander, succeeded in 498 BC by his brother Hippocrates, who defeated the troops of Syracuse at Helorus. When Hippocrates died in a battle against the Hyblaean Sicels, in 491 BC, he was succeeded by the tyrant Gelon, the head of Hippocrates' cavalry. After conquering Syracuse in 458 BC, he transferred a large part of the population of Gela there, leaving the city in a profound crisis which ended only after the fall of the Deinomenids in Syracuse, in 466 BC. In 424 BC a summit of Siceliot cities held at Gela decided that the time had come to drive back the threatening Athenian army, which had been sent to help some of them in 427 BC. The city allied with Syracuse during the Athenian expedition which ended in September 413 BC with the defeat of Athens at Helorus, and with Agrigento against the Carthaginians. Besieged by Himilco and having failed in its attempt to help the Syracusan army of Dionysius I, the city was taken and destroyed after a long siege, and the population deported to *Leontinoi.* It was repopulated in accordance with the subsequent peace treaty, and compelled to demolish all its defensive works, remaining under Carthaginian and later Syracusan rule. It rose again under Timoleon in 338 BC, extending its boundary walls over the hills of Piano Soprano and Capo Notaro, where part of the fortifications are still extant. During the tyranny of Agathocles in Syracuse, Gela suffered further destruction and pillage. Around 285 BC Phintias, a tyrant of *Akragas*, was supposed to have sent Mamertine mercenaries to destroy Gela and Camarina. Geloan refugees thus settled in the city of *Phintias*, present-day Licata.

Gela. View of the port with oil tankers.

Castle of Mussomeli.

CASTLE OF MUSSOMELI

One of the most fascinating feudal manors in Sicily, it stands on a high and rugged crag over-looking the surrounding valley. It can be reached by a path hewn out of the rock, which winds its way up to the top. The Castle consists of several constructions, the highest of which are the massive remains of a 12C fortress. In 1370 Manfredi III Chiaramonte built his Castle slightly lower down the slope. Throughout the Middle Ages this suggestive architectural complex, with its vast reception halls and service rooms, was also the symbol of the feudal power of the Chiaramonte family, which extended over a large part of Sicily. One of the four Vicars – each from an important aristocratic family – who ruled the island during the "feudal anarchy" of the 14C was a Chiaramonte. It was in this Castle that, in 1391, Manfredi gathered together the Sicilian barons struggling for autonomy. They pledged to fight against the Aragonese army which was trying to restore the Crown's authority over the island. The Castle later belonged to the Moncada, Prades, Castellar, Parapertusa, Ventimiglia, del Campo and Lanza families. It was admired as an "eagle's eyrie" by the German *Kaiser* William II Hohenzollern. Numerous legends have cast an aura of mystery over the Castle. According to one of these, the Lord of the Castle was leaving for war and, being an extremely jealous man, he decided to lock his three beautiful sisters up in a room, walling up every door and window and leaving them with some food. But when he came back, he found them dead and reduced to skeletons, with the leather of their shoes between their teeth. The war, in fact, had lasted longer than he had expected.

Enna. Aerial view of the town showing its key strategic position, with Mount Etna in the background.

ENNA

Because of its geographical position, almost in the centre of the island, Enna was once defined *umbilicus Siciliae*, as is mentioned by Cicero in his *Verrines* (IV, 107). Situated in a natural strategic position at an altitude of 931 m, it has been inhabited since prehistoric times, as the archaeolgical investigations and excavations carried out in the area have shown. According to the literature, it was first a Sican and then a Sicel centre. In 7C BC it began to assimilate Greek culture through the influence of Gela and Syracuse. It was to some extent independent until 396 BC, but as Syracusan interference increased, the city fell under the tyrant Dionysius the Elder. A Roman ally during the First Punic War, it was conquered by the Carthaginians in 259 BC but liberated the following year. During the Second Punic War the Roman consul ordered that all its citizens should be killed as a punishment for having formed an alliance with the Carthaginians (212 BC). It was at Enna that, in 136 BC, the devastating slaves' revolt led by the Syrian slave Eunus broke out, which spread throughout Sicily. Consul Rupilius besieged and took back the city in 132 BC, crushing any further attempts at rebellion. Under the Romans Enna continued to be a military fortress and the administrative centre of a vast grain-producing territory. Historical sources refer to it as a "holy city" because of the cult of Ceres, the Roman goddess of the fields and harvest depicted with her head garlanded with ears of corn and flowers, to whom Enna dedicated statues and temples. Under the Byzantines it maintained its strategic role as a military stronghold against the Arab invasion. After a prolonged siege, in 859 AD Enna fell and was sacked by the Muslim Abbâs Ibn Fadhl. The tragic news of Enna's fall spread throughout the Eastern Roman Empire, causing great dismay. In the 10C the town became the seat of an Emirate and a Muslim stronghold against the Norman conquerors, who took it in 1087, when the Arab Hammud negotiated its surrender to Roger I of Hauteville, Great Count of Sicily. The latter sent a garrison of Lombard soldiers from Apulia and Calabria to defend the area, and the citadel thus took the name of "Castello di Lombardia", or Lombardia Castle. Frederick II Hohenstaufen chose Enna as the headquarters for the repression of the Arab-Berber revolt which followed his coronation. The old Byzantine citadel was fortified, its walls were restored and new defensive works and towers were built. Enna thus regained its reputation of being an impregnable stronghold. The Emperor, who was fond of hunting, also built a *domus* on a hill outside the city walls, from which he could look down onto the strikingly beautiful surrounding area. The building, designed as an octagonal tower, is an extraordinary masterpiece of 13C architecture. In the following centuries the town was enriched with imposing churches, monasteries, convents and prestigious palaces. The interior of the Cathedral is particularly interesting. Enna was raised to the status of provincial capital in 1926. The religious celebrations of the Holy Week, attended by all the Confraternities of the town in their traditional costumes, are very suggestive.

Enna. Detail of the Lombardia Castle. Its name probably derived from a nearby Lombard quarter.

Piazza Armerina.

PIAZZA ARMERINA

The modern town lies 721 m above sea level, on the three verdant hills dominated by the mountain on which the ancient city was situated. The fertile area has been inhabited since Greek times (8C-7C BC). Substantial evidence of settlements and necropoli has been found on the *Montagna di Marzo*, on *Monte Navone* and in *contrada Casale*. The population descends in part from the Lombard groups who arrived in Sicily with the Norman army. The Arabs who were still settled in the hamlets of the surrounding countryside in the 12C were annihilated. In 1161, even the Lombard strongholds were destroyed by King William I of Hauteville in response to the rebellion of the barons against his centralizing power. The town was repopulated by Frederick II Hohenstaufen, and a new Lombard colony was led there from Piacenza by Umberto Mostacciolo. Traces of their Gallic-Italic language are still present in the local dialect. From the Monte district, the site of the earliest settlement, the town expanded over the surrounding hills between the 12C and the 15C, with a considerable urban development in the post-war period. A visit of the town should include the 14C royal castle, later transformed into a monastery, the churches and the Archaeological Museum. On 14 and 15 August, during the celebrations in honour of Maria Santissima delle Vittorie, the "*Palio dei Normanni*" is held, a re-enactment of the Norman victory over the Saracens, with parades and tournaments in periodic costume.

THE IMPERIAL "VILLA DEL CASALE" AT PIAZZA ARMERINA

In the Roman imperial age, the great villas of the imperial aristocracy were scattered throughout Sicily. These were architectural complexes which consisted of various buildings serving differ-

*Piazza Armerina.
Villa del Casale. General
view of the buildings.*

ent purposes. First of all, there was the *domus* of the lord with all the comforts of the time, including private and sometimes public thermae. Then there were dormitories for workers, servants and slaves, stables, workshops and kitchens, storehouses for the harvest and food. These "villas" were in fact situated within the large agricultural estates – the latifundia – which characterized Roman Sicily and where mainly grain was cultivated. Archaeological investigations throughout Sicily have brought to light the remains of these architectural complexes, similar to those discovered in Roman North Africa. The largest is the complex known as "Villa del Casale", but other notable remains have been found at Patti, Tellaro and Dirueli. The sumptuous complex of Piazza Armerina has been attributed to the aristocratic family of Maximianus Erculeus. It was built between the end of the 3C and the beginning of the 4C AD in the fertile valley of the Gela River, in the middle of a vast rural latifundium. According to Vinicio Gentili, the researcher who discovered the archaeological site, the Villa reached its maximum splendour between the 4C and 5C AD. The site is extremely interesting to visit because of the architectural features of the buildings and, most of all, because of the figured and ornamental mosaics which decorate all the rooms, making up the greatest mosaic series of Roman Sicily to have come down to us. One of the main subjects in these mosaics is hunting, a recurrent theme also of late-Roman figurative art in North Africa (see, for instance, the Roman mosaics reassembled in the Bardo Museum in Tunis) which was to come into fashion again in the Middle Ages (see "King Roger's Rooms" in the Royal Palace in Palermo).

Top, left:
Piazza Armerina. Villa del Casale. The large bath area of the thermae, an exedra with a semicircular tetrastyle portico and columns made of stuccoed circular bricks.

Top, right:
Piazza Armerina. Villa del Casale. The remaining marble columns of the wide atrium with arcades which was entered from three monumental doors.

"Diaeta" of the Little Hunt

Top, left: One of the five mosaic sections depicting hunting scenes in the woods of the imperial estate, the **hunting of the wild boar**. The animal, wounded by spears, is attacking a hunter accompanied by a pack of hounds.

Bottom, left: **The Cubiculum of the erotic scene**. In the middle of the laurel-framed medallion is an erotic scene depicting a crowned ephebus and a half-naked maiden.

Bottom, right: In a **"lucus Dianae"**, with a column surmounted by a statue of Artemis in the centre, a sacrificial rite is being performed in honour of the goddess of hunting. From an iconographical point of view, this is the most interesting mosaic of the Villa.

The Great Hunt Walk

Top: The great floor mosaic in the so-called "Great Hunt" covered corridor, with details illustrating the different stages of the capture, killing and transport of animals in a typically African scenery. The corridor is delimited by two exedrae on which are represented two Roman provinces. Dark Africa is symbolized by the Phoenix, the imaginary bird said to rise rejuvenated from the ashes of its burning nest. In the left exedra is perhaps the representation of Armenia, flanked by a wild bear. Between the two regions are the hunting scenes, a splendid and vivid decorative composition. While still reflecting, as a whole, the naturalistic style, the great mosaics of the Villa herald the abstract colourist style which was to open the way to Byzantinism (G. V. Gentili).

Bottom, right:
Vestibule of the small circus. Floor mosaic depicting "Children racing".

Morgantina. General view of the Agora with the theatre and the Roman gymnasium with its rooms and basins used for ablutions. In the middle is the flight of steps which led up to the Citadel quarters and was also used for public assemblies, with a podium for speakers at the east end.

MORGANTINA

Not far from the small town of Aidone is the archaeological site of Morgantina. According to Strabo, the city was founded by Morges, king of the Morgeti, people who came from southern Italy before the arrival of the Greeks. The earliest Greek settlement dates from around the mid-6C BC and was located on a steep hilly area dominating the Agora. It seems that the indigenous Morgeti did not oppose any resistance to the arrival of the Greeks, and that there was a peaceful fusion of the two cultures. Morgantina reached the height of its splendour around 300 BC, remaining for most of the time in the sphere of influence of Syracuse. Under Agathocles, the Agora was renovated. Because of its opposition to the expansionist designs of the Geloan Hippocrates, the city suffered a first severe destruction at the end of the 6C BC, followed in 459 BC by raids and pillaging by the Sicels of Ducetius, who had united in a nationalistic movement against Greek expansion. Archaeological excavations have brought to light the monumental area of the Agora and, up on the hill, the residential quarter with the remains of luxury houses with rooms arranged around a peristyle and embellished with floor and wall decorations. According to historical sources, Morgantina was an important commercial centre because of its geographical position on the road which, from the Tyrrhenian coasts and from the Aeolian islands, led southwards to the city of Agira and to the southern coasts of the island. To the east of the Agora is the horseshoe-shaped theatre, dating from the 4C BC, with sixteen tiers of seats divided into five sectors. Of great interest is the sanctuary dedicated to Persephone and Aphrodite, as is attested by terracotta offerings to Persephone and Demeter – and one to Aphrodite – unearthed in the area.

RAGUSA

The surroundings of Ragusa Ibla bear traces of human settlements dating from as early as the 9C-8C BC. Considerable evidence has been found, in particular, of indigenous villages dating from the time of Greek colonization, which compelled the Sicels to withdraw towards the uplands further inland. There they founded the city of Ibla, the *Hibla Heraia* mentioned by historical sources, a stronghold situated in the upper Irminio valley, in a fertile land with abundant supplies of water. Its closeness to the Syracusan sub-colony of Camarina, founded in 598 BC according to Thucydides, allowed Ibla to exploit the coastal trade outlets of the Greek city, establishing profitable cultural and economic relations with its population. During the lengthy and wearying Punic wars it was conquered by the Carthaginians and later by the Romans. In the 4C AD it became a Byzantine stronghold because of its strategic position. The Saracens conquered it in 868 AD. Later, in the 14C, it was ruled by Manfredi Chiaramonte and joined on to the county of Modica. In 1693 a devastating earthquake destroyed ancient Ibla, and a new town was built in baroque style on the adjacent Patro hill. In 1730 the medieval town of Ibla, where the most remarkable monuments of Ragusa are to be found, was extensively restored and rebuilt by the architect Rosario Gagliardi. It is interesting to visit the Hyblaean Archaeological Museum, established in 1961 to house the finds from the fruitful excavations carried out throughout the territory of Ragusa. The material is arranged in chronological order, from the prehistoric to the late-Roman settlements. The museum displays notable finds from archaic and classical Sicel necropoli and a rich collection of archaeological items from Hellenistic centres.

Ragusa. View of ancient Ibla with the Duomo of San Giorgio, and the 18C town stretching over Patro hill.

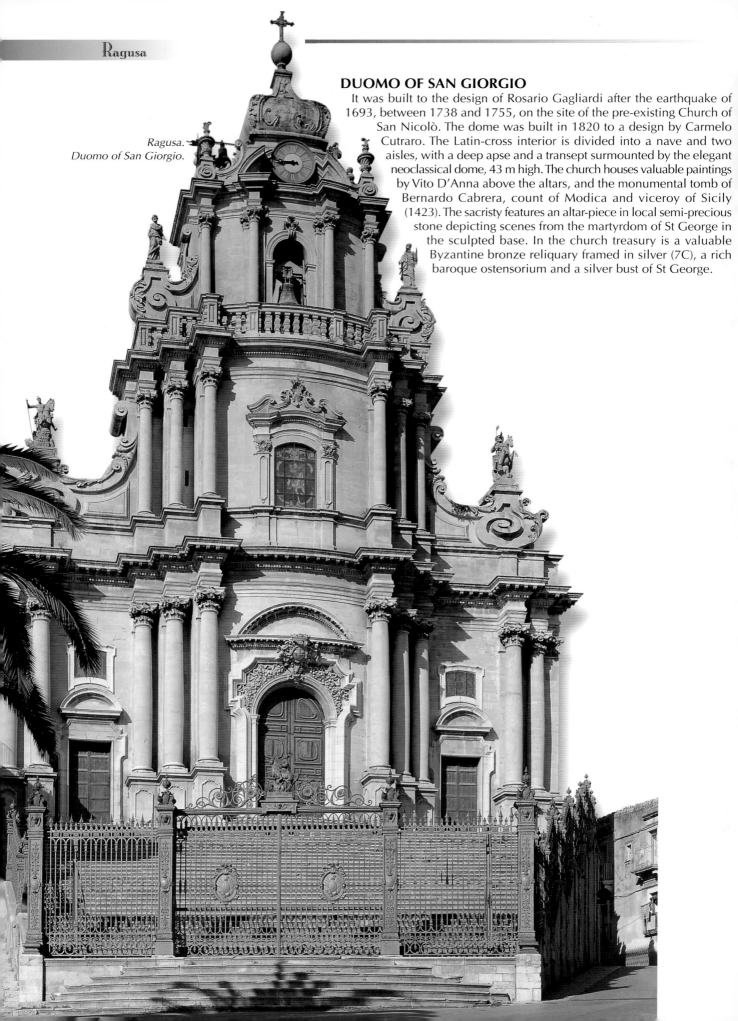

Ragusa.
Duomo of San Giorgio.

DUOMO OF SAN GIORGIO

It was built to the design of Rosario Gagliardi after the earthquake of 1693, between 1738 and 1755, on the site of the pre-existing Church of San Nicolò. The dome was built in 1820 to a design by Carmelo Cutraro. The Latin-cross interior is divided into a nave and two aisles, with a deep apse and a transept surmounted by the elegant neoclassical dome, 43 m high. The church houses valuable paintings by Vito D'Anna above the altars, and the monumental tomb of Bernardo Cabrera, count of Modica and viceroy of Sicily (1423). The sacristy features an altar-piece in local semi-precious stone depicting scenes from the martyrdom of St George in the sculpted base. In the church treasury is a valuable Byzantine bronze reliquary framed in silver (7C), a rich baroque ostensorium and a silver bust of St George.

Archaeological site of Camarina.

CAMARINA

The third Syracusan sub-colony in chronological order, Camarina was founded in 598 BC by the oecists Menecolus and Daxon. Having entered into an alliance with the Sicels and rebelled against its mother-town, it was destroyed in 553 BC. According to Herodotus, it was conquered by the Geloan Hippocrates and rebuilt in 492 BC, but was again destroyed by Gelon, a tyrant of Syracuse, who demolished its fortress and took its inhabitants to Syracuse, where they were naturalized. The city was rebuilt once more in 416 BC by Gela. It remained neutral during the Peloponnesian War and took possession of Morgantina in 424 BC, as provided for by the peace treaty signed at Gela. In the following turbulent years it was occupied by the Carthaginians in 405 BC, but rebuilt and repopulated by Timoleon in 339 BC. It was sacked by the Syracusan general Agathocles in 309 BC and by the Mamertines in 279 BC. The city suffered further destruction in 258 AD at the hands of the Romans, and was never again rebuilt.

SYRACUSE

Archaeological investigation has found evidence of human settlements dating from as early as the end of the 14C BC on the *island of Ortygia*, where the great city of Syracuse was to be founded in the 8C BC. The new settlement was established by a group of Corinthians led by Archias, who drove the previous settlers, the Sicels, back towards the Hyblaean Mountains. It took its name from a nearby marsh called Syrako. The new settlers embarked on a programme of economic and political development and territorial expansion which, within a period of 70 years, resulted in the foundation of three colonies: *Akrai* in 664 BC (the present-day Palazzolo Acreide), *Casmene* in 643 BC and *Camarina*, on the southern coast of Sicily, in 598 BC. For centuries, Syracuse was the main centre of Greek culture on the island, often in contrast with the economic and military interests of the Carthaginians. It became the greatest, richest and politically most important city of Sicily, the home of artists, scientists and fearless colonizers. A true metropolis of antiquity, it extended over a large territory, with safe and well-sheltered landing places and an excellent defensive system, its main stronghold being the Euryalus Castle, a masterpiece of ancient military art. The city was also enriched with splendid palaces, patrician houses, temples, theatres and other magnificent buildings. It allied with the Romans who, however, had to use military force to conquer it. Even under Roman rule Syracuse maintained its political, cultural and economic supremacy – indeed, it considerably increased its prestige in the Mediterranean area. The Greek Orthodox religion spread rapidly. The Byzantine administration privileged the city, assigning it a new political and administrative role. It became the capital of the *Thema* (Byzantine imperial province) of Sicily which also included Calabria and the Salento area, heralding the medieval Kingdom of Sicily. Emperor Constant decided to move his court from Constantinople to Syracuse, which also became the see of the Byzantine primate, connected with the Orthodox patriarchate of Constantinople. The Arabs besieged the city several times and finally took it by storm in 877, slaughtering its population and burning its buildings. The news of the fall of Syracuse caused great dismay throughout the Christian world. A long-established centre of Graeco-Latin civilization was thought to have faded away forever. In fact, under Arab rule the city fell into decay and seemed to vanish from history. Only in the Middle Ages did it begin to revive, particularly when Frederick II Hohenstaufen built there one of his most splendid residences, the Maniace Castle. The fact that the city had two good ports contributed to its economic recovery but at the same time attracted the ambitious designs of the Ottoman Turks, French and Barbary pirates, so the Crown built several bastions and other defensive works (on the site now occupied by the Montedoro quarter). The city was almost completely destroyed by the earthquake of 1693. It was rebuilt to a design by the royal architect Carlo de Grunenbergh, a native of Flanders who created and fortified the present-day isthmus and reorganized the city's defensive sys-

Above: Syracuse.
Regional Archaeological
Museum. Silver tetradachm
from Syracuse, signed by
Kimon (4C BC).

Below: Syracuse.
Greek Theatre.

Above: Syracuse. Roman Amphitheatre (1C AD).

Left: Syracuse. The Altar of Hieron II, a monumental altar for public sacrifices built in the 3C BC and dedicated to Zeus Eleutherios. It measures 198 x 22.80 m.

tem. In the 18C, churches, palaces, convents and houses on the island of Ortygia were rebuilt in an elegant baroque style which still characterizes this part of the city. However, Syracuse had by then decayed into a mere small fortified town compared to the other urban centres on the Ionic coast, such as Augusta, Catania and Messina, which were slowly inheriting its political and economic role. Only in the early 20C did the city flourish again, when it began to expand inland after its fortifications were demolished and the surrounding area was reclaimed. Also, and most importantly, famous archaeologists began their campaigns and surveys in the area, and Syracuse became the main centre of Sicilian archaeology.

THE GREEK THEATRE

It was built by Hieron II on the site of a pre-existing theatre whose history is associated with *Aeschylus* of Eleusis (c 524-456 BC), the first of the great Greek tragedians, *Epicharmus* (6C-5C BC), the Syracusan father of Greek comedy, and their contemporaries the playwriters *Phormides* and *Deinolochus*. This earlier theatre staged the premiere of Aeschylus' tragedy *The Persians* and, in 476 BC, *The Women of Etna*, written to celebrate the foundation of the city of Etna by Hieron I, known as "the Etnean". The name of the architect who designed the earlier theatre was Demokopos, as is reported by the mime-writer Sophron (late 5C BC). In Roman times the theatre was altered to adapt it to the performance of circus and water games. In the 16C the ancient stones of the theatre, amphitheatre and the Altar of Hieron II were used to build the fortifications on the island of Ortygia, thus suffering the same fate as many other monuments of ancient Sicily.

THE ROMAN AMPHITHEATRE

This majestic construction, dating from the 1C AD, is one of the largest among the late Roman amphitheatres of Catania, Pompei and Pola. Elliptical in plan, it measures 140 x 119 m in the external diameter and 70 x 40 m in the arena, with a central cistern supplied by two canals. Its lower part was carved from the rock, in accordance with Syracusan tradition. The tiers of seats were originally covered with slabs of stone in order to prevent their deterioration. At the end of the longer axis, two entrances led into the arena, the main entrance being originally on the south side. At the foot of the steps there was a vaulted corridor for the entrance of wild animals and gladiators who took part in the bloody performances held in the arena.

Opposite page, top: Syracuse. The Ear of Dionysius.

Left: Syracuse. Roman tomb with overhang, known as the "tomb of Archimedes".

Below: Syracuse. Temple of Apollo (6C BC).

THE EAR OF DIONYSIUS

This artificial cave, 65 m long and 23 m high, owes its name to *Michelangelo Merisi*, known as *Caravaggio*, who visited it as well as the *Latomie del Paradiso* in 1586, accompanied by the Syracusan archaeologist Vincenzo Mirabella, and noticed its human ear-shaped entrance. The legend thus began to circulate that Dionysius had excavated the cave to use it as a prison, and that he exploited its amazing acoustics to eavesdrop on his prisoners.

Syracuse. Euryalus Castle. The courtyard, the very heart of the defensive system, with three of the five original towers. From the vast square surrounded by various buildings, a series of underground passages enabled soldiers to make sorties outside when necessary. Over the centuries, the fortress was altered to adapt it to the new defensive systems, until the Roman conquest in 212 BC. In Byzantine times it was partially rebuilt to protect the city against Arab attacks.

THE TEMPLE OF APOLLO (Apolloyon)

Dating from the early 6C BC, it is considered the oldest Doric peripteral temple in Sicily. It measures 58.10 x 24.50 m, and had 17 columns on the sides and 6 on the fronts. The cella was divided into aisles by two rows of double-order columns. Its archaic character can be seen in the design of the columns and in the width of the intercolumns. The temple has been altered and adapted over the centuries. It was transformed into a Christian church in Byzantine times, into a mosque under the Muslims, and into a Christian basilica again in the Middle Ages. In the 16C it became a Spanish barracks known as the "Old Quarter".

THE EURYALUS CASTLE

The castle took its name from the morphology of the land on which it was erected (from the Greek *eurvelos*, i.e. broad-based nail). This remarkable archaeological site is one of the most extraordinary examples of ancient Greek military architecture. The complex, situated at the top of the Epipolae, was crossed by the road which linked Syracuse to its inland territories. During the Athenian siege of the city (415-413 BC) the plateau had not yet been fortified and was one of the weak points of the Syracusan defensive system. It was on this occasion that the need was felt to build a massive stronghold to protect the city against enemy attacks. Ordered by Dionysius the Elder and built in six years, from 402 to 397 BC, the formidable construction frustrated all Carthaginian attempts to conquer the city.

THE CIANE SPRING
AND THE FOUNTAIN OF ARETHUSA

The Greek name of the Ciane River derives from the colour of its waters (*cyanos*, blue) or, more poetically, from the myth of Cyane. The daughter of Cyanippus, Bacchus' priest in Syracuse, Cyane was with Proserpina when the latter was abducted by Pluto. As a punishment for having tried to prevent the rape of Proserpina, the god of the Underworld turned her into a spring. A Natural Reserve has recently been established to preserve the environmental wealth of the river, the only one in Europe where papyrus plants still grow wild.

Arethusa, a nymph of Artemis and the daughter of Nereus and Doris, is a mythological figure associated with the origins of Syracuse. According to legend, one day Arethusa, seeking refreshment after hunting, bathed in the river Alpheus who, struck with love for the beautiful nymph, took on human form to pursue her. In order to protect Arethusa, Artemis turned her into a spring flowing underground which emerges on the islet of Ortygia.

Above: The Fountain of Arethusa with the luxuriant papyrus plants.

Left: The luxuriant banks of the Ciane River.

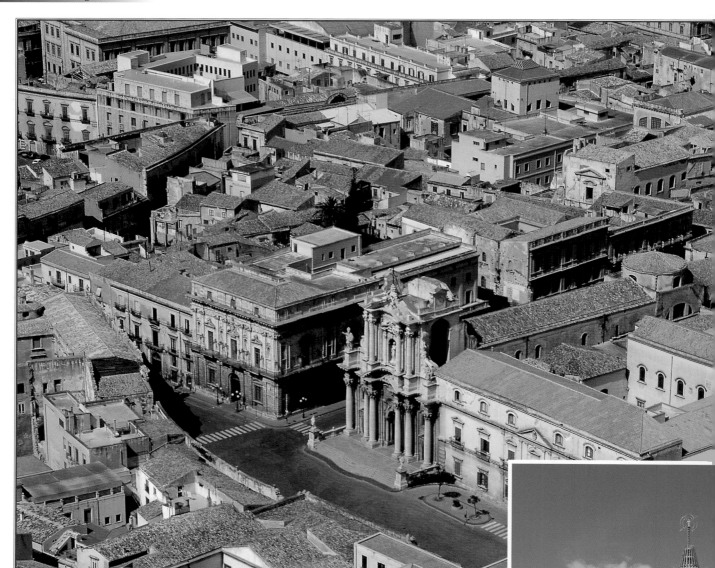

Above: Syracuse. The Duomo.

THE DUOMO

In Sicilian ancient and medieval history, it often occurred that religious buildings passed from one cult to another, as also happened in other regions of the Mediterranean. The Temple of Athena (Athenaion) was built in the 7C BC on the highest point of the islet of Ortygia, and restored by the Deinomenids in the 5C BC. It was transformed into a church in the early days of Christianity, and into a mosque during Arab rule, to be consecrated again to the Christian cult in 1093. The façade, destroyed during the earthquake of 1693, was rebuilt to a design by Andrea Palma between 1725 and 1753. In 1925 the church was restored, and ten Doric columns from the Temple of Athena were embedded into the walls of the left aisle.

THE SANCTUARY
OF THE MADONNA DELLE LACRIME

On the morning of 29 August 1953, a small plaster image of the Virgin Mary in the house of Angelo Iannuso and Antonina Giusto suddenly began to shed tears. On the following days, 30 and 31 August and again on 1 September, tears were again seen on the Virgin's face. This extraordinary phenomenon turned the house of the two simple workers into a sort of sanctuary which attracted crowds of believers wishing to see and touch the tears flowing down from the clear eyes of the Virgin. A commission appointed by the archiepiscopal Curia ascertained that the tears were human. On 19 May 1954 Cardinal Ruffini, the Archbishop of Palermo, laid the foundation stone of the Sanctuary of the Madonna delle Lacrime (Our Lady of the Tears), built to a design by two French architects, Michel Andrault and Pierre Parat. On 29 August 1968 the sacred image of the Virgin was displayed in the Crypt, which was opened on 1 September. Now it is exhibited in the upper part of the building, completed in 1990.

Above: Syracuse. Sanctuary of the Madonna delle Lacrime.

Bottom, left: Syracuse. The spire of the Sanctuary of the Madonna delle Lacrime, 94.30 m high. Eighteen doorways lead into the Crypt, which can contain 3,000 people. The upper church covers a surface area of 4,700 sq m and can contain 11,000 people.

Bottom, right: Syracuse. Madonna delle Lacrime.

95

Right: Syracuse. Regional Archaeological Museum. Venus Anadyomene, also known as "Venus Landolina" from the name of the archaeologist Saverio Landolina, who discovered it in a nymphaeum in the Achradina quarter, in Syracuse.

Bottom: Syracuse. Regional Archaeological Museum. Black- and red-figured Attic vase (5C BC).

THE "PAOLO ORSI" REGIONAL ARCHAEOLOGICAL MUSEUM

The museum is dedicated to the great archaeologist Paolo Orsi (1859-1935), who set up the former Archaeological Museum in Piazza Duomo. Built in the park of Villa Landolina between 1967 and 1988 to a design by the architect Franco Minissi, the new building is the most important and innovative archaeological museum in Sicily and one of the foremost in Europe. In its 9,000 sq m of exhibition space set out on two floors, it displays 18,000 archaeological finds from the city of Syracuse and from the eastern regions of the island. The chronological succession of exhibits in the various sectors starts from the prehistoric and protohistoric ages and continues with the Copper Age and different stages of the Bronze (early, middle, and late) and Iron Ages. The following sectors feature material from the first Greek colonies of Naxos, Mylai, Zancle, Katane and Leontinoi, the largest space being devoted to the

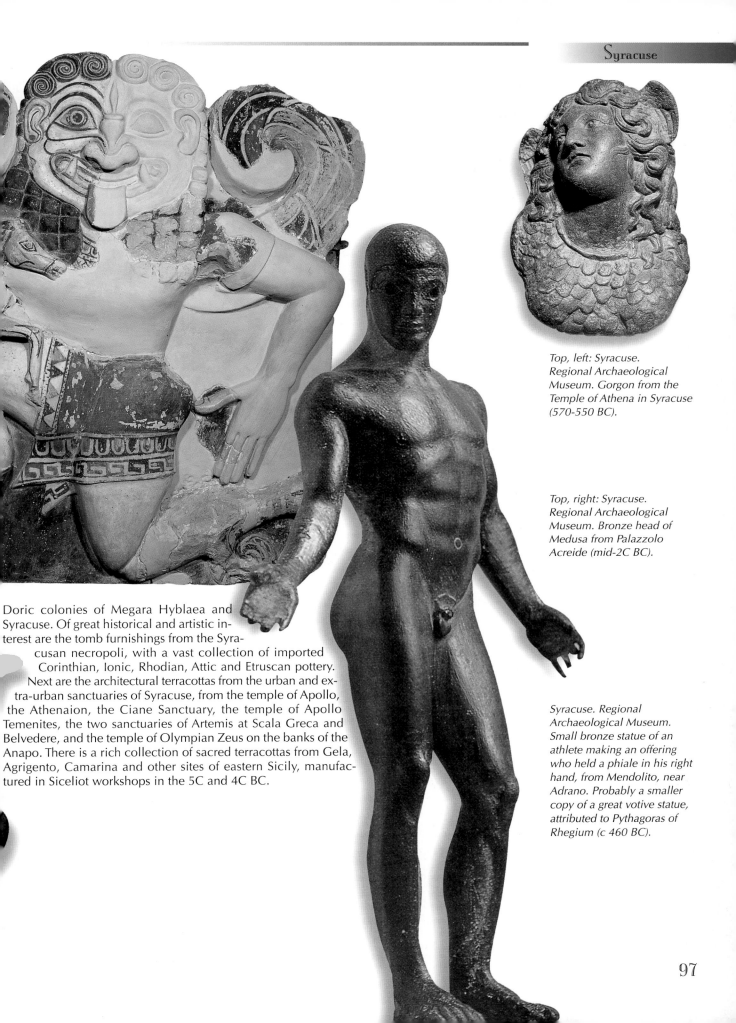

Top, left: Syracuse.
Regional Archaeological
Museum. Gorgon from the
Temple of Athena in Syracuse
(570-550 BC).

Top, right: Syracuse.
Regional Archaeological
Museum. Bronze head of
Medusa from Palazzolo
Acreide (mid-2C BC).

Doric colonies of Megara Hyblaea and
Syracuse. Of great historical and artistic in-
terest are the tomb furnishings from the Syra-
cusan necropoli, with a vast collection of imported
Corinthian, Ionic, Rhodian, Attic and Etruscan pottery.
Next are the architectural terracottas from the urban and ex-
tra-urban sanctuaries of Syracuse, from the temple of Apollo,
the Athenaion, the Ciane Sanctuary, the temple of Apollo
Temenites, the two sanctuaries of Artemis at Scala Greca and
Belvedere, and the temple of Olympian Zeus on the banks of the
Anapo. There is a rich collection of sacred terracottas from Gela,
Agrigento, Camarina and other sites of eastern Sicily, manufac-
tured in Siceliot workshops in the 5C and 4C BC.

Syracuse. Regional
Archaeological Museum.
Small bronze statue of an
athlete making an offering
who held a phiale in his right
hand, from Mendolito, near
Adrano. Probably a smaller
copy of a great votive statue,
attributed to Pythagoras of
Rhegium (c 460 BC).

Noto. Church of San Francesco, designed by the architect Rosario Gagliardi, and the side of the Santissimo Salvatore convent with its pointed tower.

NOTO

Ancient Noto, a Sicel indigenous centre, was situated on the Meti hill, 152 m above sea level. It was inhabited since prehistoric times, as is testified by the numerous necropoli and the substantial archaeological finds from the "Castelluccio culture" (17C-15C BC) and the "Finocchito culture" (8C-7C BC). In the 3C BC the ancient *Neai* underwent considerable development under Hieron II. In Roman times it became a *civitas decumana* and enjoyed special privileges. It was conquered by the Arabs in 866 AD, and raised to the status of capital of the vast Val di Noto department. From the 12C – except for short periods of feudal submission – it was a city of the royal domain, entrusted with the administration of vast territories, and enjoyed considerable economic and commercial prosperity. Talented men of culture were born in Noto, including the humanist Giovanni Aurispa, the architect Matteo Carnelivari and the jurist Andrea Barbagio. In the 16C and 17C the transformation of the medieval town began, but was brusquely interrupted by the earthquake of 1693. Following the disastrous event, Giuseppe Lanza, duke of Camastra and the royal official in charge of

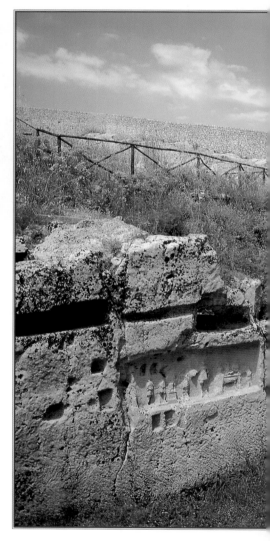

the reconstruction work, decided that the new town should be built on a different site.

Renowned architects and engineers participated in its construction, including Rosario Gagliardi, Paolo Labisi, Carlo de Grünenberg, Vincenzo Sinatra, Antonio Mazza and a skilful group of master stonemasons who, in the course of the 18C, created an urban and monumental site of outstanding artistic value.

PALAZZOLO ACREIDE (Akrai)

Substantial traces of prehistoric human settlements have been found in the surroundings of the present-day town. In 664 BC Syracuse, pursuing its intense expansionist policy towards the interior, founded its first sub-colony, Akrai. The road which led to the new city was of vital strategic importance for communications between Syracuse and the Greek cities on the southern coast via Selinunte. Under the Romans, after 214 BC, it was a *civitas stipendiaria* and continued to prosper thanks to its fertile agricultural land. Destroyed by the Arabs, it flourished again in the Middle Ages. Archaeological excavations in ancient Akrai have brought to light the Greek theatre, dating from the 3C BC, a small but well-preserved building with a semicircular cavea divided into 9 wedges and 12 tiers which could seat about 600 people. The Latomie dell'Intagliata and dell'Intagliatella can also be visited, which are stone quarries from the Greek age with rock carvings, used for worship of the Heroes. Above the Latomie are the foundations of a Greek archaic temple, probably dedicated to Aphrodite.

Above: Palazzolo Acreide. Greek Theatre (3C BC).

Centre: Palazzolo Acreide. Latomie dell'Intagliata and dell'Intagliatella.

Catania. Aerial view of the city centre, with the Church of San Francesco (in the foreground) and, higher up, the imposing Cathedral and the dome of Saint Agatha's Abbey (1735-67), the work of G. B. Vaccarini.

CATANIA

"Thucles and the Chalcidians set out from Naxos five years after the foundation of Syracuse, drove out the Sicels by arms and founded Leontini and afterwards Catania, the Catanians themselves choosing Evarchus as their founder". (Thucydides, Book IV, 3).

We thus learn that Katane, present-day Catania, was founded by Chalcidian colonists shortly after 729 BC, during the earliest stage of Greek colonization in Sicily. The territory was formerly inhabited by the Sicels from central and southern Italy who, during the Bronze Age, had in turn driven Sican settlers westwards. Katane and the other Chalcidian cities, founded in the valley crossed by the Simeto River, lived in harmony with each other and with the Sicel populations of the surrounding territories, until Hieron I, a tyrant of Syracuse, came to power. In 476 BC he transplanted the populations of Naxos and Katane to Leontini and "re-founded" Katane under a new name, Etna, bringing settlers from the Peloponnesus and introducing his son Deinomenes as its ruler. This tragic event provided the main theme for Pindar's "First Pithian" and was also narrated by Aeschylus in his play "The Women of Etna" (c 470 BC), unfortunately lost. In 461 BC, following a Sicel-Syracusan attack, the population of Etna was forced to seek refuge on Sicel territory, at Inessa, which was renamed Etna. Katane, repopulated by the groups formerly expelled by Hieron and by new Syracusan and Sicel settlers, reassumed its original name. A great figure in the city's history, albeit one that is slightly exaggerated by the legends, was the lawgiver Charondas, the author of a written code of law which was to be adopted by other Greek-Sicilian cities of Chalcidian origin. However, the exact period in which he lived has not yet been ascertained. In 263 BC, during the Second Punic War, Katane was conquered by the Romans and renamed Catina. After 210 BC, when the entire island was under Roman rule, the devastated cities and rural areas called for quick and extensive reconstruction, which the *Pax Romana* contributed to attain. Throughout the Republican and Imperial ages Catina thus became a prosperous city, as is attested by historical sources and by the considerable number of Roman buildings that have been brought to light in the area, although it was destroyed in 123 by a terrible eruption of Mount Etna, as mentioned by the Christian historian P. Orosio. The Romans privileged the city and built imposing public buildings – the remains of which can still be seen – including aqueducts, thermae, theatres, amphitheatres, naumachies, gymnasiums, odeums, triumphal arches. The city continued to flourish in the Byzantine age thanks to maritime trade. Seriously damaged, sacked and depopulated by the Arabs, it slowly recovered in the Middle Ages, when Emperor Frederick II Hohenstaufen built there one of his most prestigious castles, known as the Ursino Castle, designed by the royal architect Riccardo da Lentini. In the 14C the castle was often the seat of the Aragonese sovereigns of Sicily. In the following centuries the city continued to prosper, mainly thanks to the enterprising nature of its inhabitants and

to the cultural activities of the *Studium Urbis*, the first Sicilian university, founded in 1434 by King Alfonso "the Magnanimous" (of Sicily and Aragon), arousing the envy of Palermo and Messina. Unfortunately, in the 17C it experienced two disastrous events. The first was the eruption of Mount Etna in 1669, when an enormous lava stream flowed into the west side of the city as far as the port, which was considerably transformed. The second was the terrible earthquake of 11 January 1693, which razed the city to the ground, causing the death of 16,000 people, that is two thirds of its population. Catania gathered up all its strength to react to these two natural disasters, and rose again from its ruins, greater and more beautiful than before, thanks to the administrative ability of the royal officials entrusted with the reconstruction work, led by the Duke of Camastra, lieutenant to the king, and to the skill of architects and builders such as G. B. Vaccarini, G. Palazzotto, A. Amato, A. Italia, S. Ittar and others. The elegant baroque style of churches and palaces in the old city centre still bears witness to the successful reconstruction work carried out in the 18C. In spite of the considerable damage caused by bombings during World War II, in the last few decades Catania has gained new prestige thanks to the entrepreneurship of its inhabitants.

Catania. The Swabian Ursino Castle, housing the Civic Museum. Built by Frederick II of Swabia between 1239 and 1250, the castle originally stood on a promontory jutting out into the sea, but a lava mass during the eruption of 1669 surrounded it, separating it from the coast.

THE URSINO CASTLE

This is one of the most famous of the castles built by Emperor Frederick II Hohenstaufen in the Kingdom of Sicily, which were mainly used as residences by the sovereign when travelling through his vast territories with his court. The Ursino Castle, designed and built by the royal architect Riccardo da Lentini, is characterized by a regular plan like its counterparts at Augusta and Syracuse.

Catania. The monumental façade of the Church of San Nicolò, begun in 1687 by G. B. Contini. For various reasons, its construction was carried on discontinuously until 1796, when C. Battaglia Sant'Angelo started work again, only to leave it incomplete. Today it is used as a "Chapel to the Fallen".

It owes its name to one of its later owners. The castle was originally situated near the port, on a promontory overlooking the city, but the enormous lava flow produced by the eruption of Mount Etna in 1669 filled the surrounding low-lying areas and poured into the port, altering its altitude vis-à-vis the city. It is now the seat of the Civic Museum.

CHURCH OF SAN NICOLO'

The peculiar charm of this construction is not only due to its majestic proportions, but also to the fact that it was left unfinished. Besides, the harmonious plastic architectural features of the façade give it a very "dramatic" effect. The Latin-cross interior is divided into a nave and two aisles by massive columns. The transept covers a surface area of 105 x 48 m, and the dome is 62 m high. The monumental construction was begun in 1687 by G. B. Contini, interrupted by the earthquake of 1693 and carried on discontinuously until 1796, when C. Battaglia Santangelo started work again, however leaving it incomplete. Today it is used as a "Chapel to the Fallen".

THE CATHEDRAL

It was built between 1078 and 1093 by the Great Count Roger I of Hauteville, on the site and remains of the Roman imperial *Thermae of Achilles*. It was originally a fortified church, as can be seen from the transept, with its few single- and double-light windows, and from the battlemented top. Material from Roman imperial buildings was used for its construction. The main body and the façade were designed by Giovan Battista Vaccarini and built between 1733 and 1761. The dome was constructed in the last decade of the 18C to a design by Antonio Battaglia. The bell tower, built in 1868 by Carmelo Sciuto Patti, is a reconstruction of the 15C original, which collapsed onto the nave and aisles during the earthquake of 1693. The reconstruction project was drawn up by the architect Girolamo Palazzotto. The interior reflects the aesthetic canons of 18C architecture. Divided by pillars into a nave and two aisles, it has retained its original medieval style in the transept and apses. Placed against one of the pillars of the nave is the monumental tomb with the remains of the great Catania-born composer *Vincenzo Bellini*, transferred there in 1876 from the Père Lachaise cemetery in Paris. The tomb is the work of Giovan Battista Tassara. The cathedral is dedicated to the patron saint of the city, St Agatha, a virgin from Catania martyred in 250 AD under Emperor Decius. Every year, on 5 November, a solemn ceremony is held in her honour. In the sacellum of the right apse are the *relics* of the saint and the valuable *treasury of St Agatha*, including the valuable "Shrine", a large reliquary in embossed wrought silver decorated with statues of saints, designed and begun by Antonio La Nuara in 1460-1476, resumed and completed in 1572 by Sicilian artists such as Lattari, De Mauro, P. Guarna, Vincenzo and Antonio Archifel.

Catania. The Cathedral and the Elephant Fountain, by G. B. Vaccarini (1763). The base on which the Elephant stands is decorated with sculpted allegories of the Simeto and Amenano rivers and with putti pouring water into the basins below.

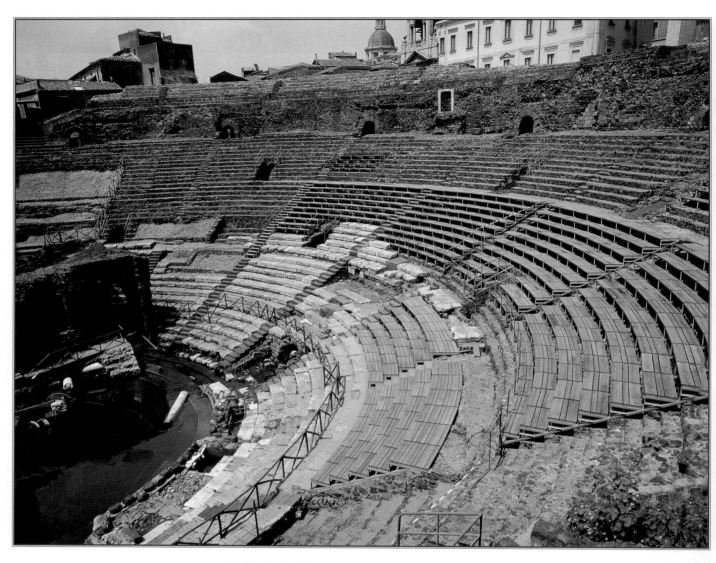

Above: Catania. The cavea of the Roman Theatre.

Right: Catania. The orchestra of the Roman Theatre, with the foundations flooded by the waters of the Amenano.

*Catania. Piazza Stesicoro
with the remains
of the Amphitheatre.*

THE ROMAN THEATRE

It was built in the Augustan age at the foot of the ancient Greek Acropolis, probably on the remains of an earlier theatre. Archaeological excavations carried out in the 18C brought to light architectural marble fragments from the stage, stone inscriptions and remains of statues, which are now exhibited in the Civic Museum at the Ursino Castle. The theatre, which could seat about 7,000 people, had a diameter of 87 m (29 m in the orchestra). The cavea, divided into 9 wedges with a two-stepped enclosure, was surrounded by three ambulatories, the highest and most imposing of which formed the base of the flight of steps of the *summa cavea*. Water from the subterranean course of the Amenano River often emerges from the ground in the orchestra, forming a pool and flooding the structures.

THE ROMAN AMPHITHEATRE

This imposing construction dates from the Imperial age, probably from the 2C AD. Elliptic in plan, it measures 125 m and 105 in the longer and shorter axes respectively. With its arena measuring 71 x 51 m, it was second in size only to the Colosseum in Rome. It had 32 tiers of seats, with a total capacity of about 16,000. The steps were cut into lava stone, and part of the building was faced with marble and granite.

THE "VINCENZO BELLINI" MUSEUM

The house where the renowned composer was born and lived until a young man is now a museum with mementoes and relics relating to his life and work.

Vincenzo Bellini was born in Catania in 1801, the son of Rosario and Agata Ferlito. His first teacher was his father, an organist, choir-master and sacred music composer. At the very early age of 6, he wrote his first composition, showing a real talent for music. His paternal grandfather Vincenzo Tobia, himself an organist and composer, was also his teacher.

Bellini soon displayed his versatile gift for music, composing sacred and secular works which he played on church organs and in the "high society salons" of the city. The Municipality of Catania, in 1819, financed his studies at the conservatory of Naples, granting him a scholarship.

In Naples he had important maestros as his teachers, such as Furno, G. Tritto and Zingarelli. He continued to compose chamber and sacred music, and published his first work, a romance entitled "*Dolente Immagine*".

In 1825 he completed his studies composing the semiseria "*Adelson e Salvini*", which was so successful that he was commissioned to write an opera for the San Carlo royal theatre, "*Bianca e Fernando*" (1826). The following year he was engaged by the theatrical impresario Domenico Barbaja and composed "*Il Pirata*" for La Scala in Milan, a work in which the features of his melodramatic production were first shown.

In 1827 his unrequited love for Maddalena Fumaroli led him to settle in Milan, where he began a fruitful collaboration with the librettist Felice Romani, which was to last until his penultimate work, "*Beatrice di Tenda*".

His immortal works were all composed in eight years, from 1827 to 1835 when, after a short

Catania. Teatro Massimo
Vincenzo Bellini.

stay in London, he died in Paris of an intestinal disease which had long been afflicting him. A musical genius of Italian Romanticism, Bellini thus wrote of himself: *"… I have resolved to write few scores, no more than one a year, and I shall dedicate myself entirely to these, as I am convinced that their success will depend in large part on the choice of a captivating subject, on warm expressions, on the conflict of passions"*.

Bellini's works, known and performed all over the world, reflect the expressive strength of his soul. This is particularly evident in the dramatic accents of his *"I Puritani"* and *"Suoni la tromba e intrepido"*.

After *"Il Pirata"* (1827), Bellini composed his great works *"La Straniera"* (1829), *"I Capuleti e i Montecchi"* (1830), *"La Sonnambula"* (1831), *"Norma"* (1832) and *"I Puritani"* shortly before his death (1835).

TEATRO MASSIMO VINCENZO BELLINI

The main opera house in Catania, dedicated to Vincenzo Bellini, the Teatro Massimo was inaugurated on 31 May 1890 with the performance of Bellini's *"Norma"*. In 1812 the construction was first commissioned to the Maltese architect Zahara Buda. Work was begun but then interrupted, and the sum destined to the theatre was allocated for the building of an outer breakwater in the port of Catania, to protect it against the frequent raids by Algerian pirates in the Ionian Sea. As the original project was lost, in 1841 a new project was commissioned by the Senate of Catania to the architect Carlo Sama.

The theatre reflects Sama's eclecticism and architectural elegance both from the decorative and the functional-acoustic points of view. The magnificent auditorium has four tiers of boxes and a gallery with a frescoed ceiling by Ernesto Bellandi, depicting *Bellini's Apotheosis* and allegories of his *Norma, I Puritani, La Sonnambula* and *Il Pirata*. The curtain, by G. Sciuti, celebrates the victory of Catania over the Libyans.

Opposite page, top: Catania. V. Bellini Museum. Oil portrait of Vincenzo Bellini as a young man.

Opposite page, bottom: Catania. V. Bellini Museum. Room C with the showcases exhibiting a rich collection of photographs relating to Bellini's life, autographed letters, the original documents regarding his death at Puteaux, the death certificate and the medical post-mortem report. There is also a collection of portraits of orchestra conductors, famous opera singers such as Malibran and Turina, relatives and friends of the great composer.

Above: Panorama of Aci Trezza, the mythical scene of the Homeric legend of Ulysses.

THE RIVIERA OF THE CYCLOPS: ACI TREZZA – ACI CASTELLO – CAPO MULINI

Aci Trezza is the mythical scene of the Homeric legend of Ulysses. The rocks rising from the sea not far from the shore are the Rocks of the Cyclops which Polyphemus, blinded by Ulysses, is said to have hurled at the fleeing hero. Aci Trezza is also renowned as the scene of the famous novel *"I Malavoglia"* (The House by the Medlar Tree) by Giovanni Verga (Catania 1840-1922), the great theorist of Italian literary Verism, a style connected with European Positivism and French Naturalism of which he was a major exponent in Sicily, together with Luigi Capuana (Mineo 1839 – Catania 1915) and Federico De Roberto (Naples 1861 – Catania 1927).

Aci Castello is the site of a medieval castle built in lava stone blocks on the top of a prism-shaped basaltic lava crag. The castle was erected in 1076 by Roger of Lauria, Grand Admiral to the king of Sicily.

The rocky cliff of *Capo Mulini* reveals the natural beauty of this stretch of Sicilian coast, characterized by sharp contours and sheltered coves which are now renowned and busy bathing resorts.

Below: Aci Castello with the Norman castle erected in 1076 by Roger of Lauria. Built in lava stone blocks, it stands on the top of a basaltic prism-shaped lava crag.

MOUNT ETNA

Mount Etna is the highest volcano in Europe and one of the most active in the world. Its majestic and imposing mass, about 3,300 m high and covering a surface area of 1,600 sq km, rises up from the valley enclosed by the Alcantara and Simeto rivers in the Catania plain, overlooking the Ionian Sea in the mythological scenery of the *Riviera of the Cyclops*. Its impressive landscape stirred the imagination of the ancients and inspired their myths as well as the works of great authors of all time. The Greeks regarded it as the forge of *Hephaestus*, identified with the Roman god Vulcan, and as the house of the most tremendous of the Giants, Enceladus, the son of Uranus and Gaea, who fomented the war of the Giants against Zeus and was thrown by the Lord of Olympus into the heart of the volcano, from whence he still hurls fire at the sky. This mythological episode

The imposing mass of Mount Etna.

is taken from the *Gigantomachy*, narrating the war of the Giants against the Olympian gods, of chaos against divine order.

The most interesting natural, historical and artistic itinerary, 135 km long, starts from Catania passing through all the small towns situated on the slopes of the volcano, following a ring-like route which leads back to the city. From the northern suburbs of Catania, the coastal road leads to the picturesque centres of Aci Castello, with the medieval castle built in 1076, Aci Trezza, famous as the scene of the legendary adventures of *Ulysses* and of Verga's novel "*I Malavoglia*", and Acireale, the Roman Akis sung by Ovid and Virgil, with its magnificent 17C monuments and the famous *Santa Venera Spa*, whose therapeutic waters were used by the Greeks and the Romans. The route goes on to Giarre and Riposto, then to Fiumefreddo di Sicilia, the ancient *Flumen frigidum*, where the road starts climbing up the lower slopes of Mount Etna, passing through Calatabiano and Linguaglossa, a holiday and winter sports resort. After a visit to the *Alcantara Gorge*, the route leads to Randazzo, 765 m above sea level, a town almost entirely built of lava stone, rich in medieval monuments. Leaving Randazzo, with a view of the majestic Mount Etna, the road leads to the northern ski slopes of Piano Provenzano, 1,800 m above sea level.

Top: A picturesque view of the ski slopes on Mount Etna.

Above: An eruption.

MESSINA

The great Greek historian Thucydides reported thus on the foundation of *Zancle* (present-day Messina): *"Zancle was originally founded by pirates from Cuma, the Chalcidian town in the country of the Opicans; afterwards, however, large numbers came from Chalcis and the rest of Euboea, and helped to people the place"*. According to Strabo *"Messene was founded by the Messenians of the Peloponnesus, who named it after themselves, changing its name; for formerly it was called Zancle, on account of the crookedness of the coast"* (anything crooked was called *"Zanclion"*). An ally of Syracuse against Carthage, the city was destroyed by the Carthaginians in 396 BC and later rebuilt by Dionysius of Syracuse. At the beginning of the First Punic War it was a Roman military base. The most prosperous period thus began for the city, on account of its strategic position on the road network linking Sicily to the Tyrrhenian and Ionian coasts on the Italian mainland. Cicero, who visited Messina while preparing his case against Verres for having plundered various Sicilian cities, defined it *"Civitas maxima et locupletissima"*. Under Augustus it was raised to the privileged status of *oppidum civium romanorum*, a city administered by means of its own statutes. After the fall of the Western Roman Empire in 476 AD, Vandal and Goth invasions ushered in a period of gloom for the city, which ended with the arrival of the Byzantines. The activities of the

Aerial view of Messina and of the stele erected in 1934 on the ancient fort of San Salvatore, surmounted by a statue of the "Madonna of the Letter", with the inscription "Vos et ipsam civitatem benedicimus" taken from the letter which, according to tradition, the Virgin sent to the population of Messina in 42 AD.

As in ancient times, Messina is a key city on the road network linking Sicily to the mainland. Today a ferry service is provided both by the Italian Railways and private companies. Right: The railway and maritime station of the Italian Railways, handling intense passenger and commercial traffic.

port were revived and the city recovered its original role as a key port of call in the trade relations between the Tyrrhenian and Ionian Seas and between East and West. It resisted Muslim invasion until its fall in 843 AD. However, part of its population fled to Rometta and put up a fierce resistance, which lasted more than a century. The Normans, urged by the population to intervene against the Muslims, occupied Messina in 1061, and a period of economic and urban development began for the city. The Royal Palace, the Duomo and the Arsenal were built, and the city layout was reorganized. This 'building fever' attracted people from Amalfi, Pisa, Genoa, Florence, but also groups of Greeks, Flemish, Albanians and Armenians. The Hauteville and Hohenstaufen dynasties were succeeded by the "*evil Angevin rule*", as Dante defined it. The anti-Angevin uprisings in Palermo and the subsequent War of the Sicilian Vespers caused great suffering to Messina which, being a strategic city, was besieged by Charles of Anjou. The population, led by Alaimo, fought bravely against the French troops. The figures of two heroines emerged, Dina and Clarenza, now celebrated by two statues on the bell tower of the Duomo, which depict them in the act of ringing the bells of the city revolt. In 1535 Messina triumphantly welcomed Emperor Charles V after his conquest of Tunis and, later, Don John of Austria after his victory at Lepanto against the Turks (1572). The city, which had been intended to become the capital of the Kingdom, rebelled against the Crown and passed over to France in 1674, but it was reconquered by the Spanish and suffered a violent repression which caused severe damage and depopulation. In 1743 a plague epidemic killed more than 40,000 people. An earthquake in 1783 caused further deaths and destruction. In 1908 another earthquake, probably the most disastrous natural event suffered by the city, killed 60,000 people. The pitiless American bombings of 1943 caused considerable damage, but the city once again rose from its ruins thanks to the tenacity of its inhabitants.

Top: Messina. Church of the Santissima Annunziata dei Catalani. The original apse and external transept which, together with the cylindrical cupola, were left unaltered by the 13C restructuring work.

CHURCH OF THE SANTISSIMA ANNUNZIATA DEI CATALANI

According to some scholars, this church was built between the end of the 12C and the first half of the 13C, but the exact date of construction is still controversial. It was entrusted to the Dominicans, and later to a confraternity of Catalans living in Messina. Little is also known about its original form. It was probably designed as a central-plan building, and some alterations were made in its front part. Others have suggested that the original nave and aisles were shortened. The external parts of the vaults and dome are covered with tiles. The cylindrical drum of the dome and the external walls of the transept are decorated with small blind arches featuring multicoloured ashlars and supported by small elegant columns. Stone inlays and majolicas enrich the frames running along the rear part of the church and the top of the blind arches. The building is a true architectural jewel, built in the purest Byzantine style typical of southern Italy and of the Messina area. Not far from the church is the bronze statue of Don John of Austria, celebrating his victory against the Ottoman Turks in the naval battle off Lepanto (1572).

Bottom: Messina. Fountain of Neptune.

THE DUOMO

The most prestigious medieval monument in the city, it was begun in the first half of the 12C by Roger II of Hauteville. It was consecrated in 1197 in the presence of Henry IV Hohenstaufen and dedicated to the Virgin Mary (Santa Maria). The history of the church is marked by a series of disastrous events. In 1254 a fire destroyed the painted beams of the ceiling. In 1693 it was damaged by the earthquake which also destroyed other Sicilian cities. In 1783 another terrible earthquake destroyed the walls of the transept and the bell tower. The earthquake of 1908 caused the final blow, and the church was almost completely destroyed. A reconstruction project was drawn up in 1919, and the church was reopened to the cult on 13 August 1929. In 1943 indiscriminate American bombings caused death and destruction throughout the city. 94% of the buildings were damaged or razed to the ground, and the Duomo was further damaged by a fire. Many works of art were destroyed, including the sarcophagi of Conrad IV Hohenstaufen, king of Sicily from 1250 to 1254, and Alfonso "the Magnanimous" (of Sicily and Aragon), who reigned from 1416 to 1458; the mosaic decorations; the bronze baldachin; the frescoes by G. B. Quagliata; the wooden choir and the marble inlaid floor. The church was reconstructed in the post-war period. The basilican-plan interior is divided into a nave and two aisles by two rows of 26 monolithic columns, and has three apses. The transept is covered by trusses decorated with figures of saints, angels, apostles and evangelists. The main portal was sculpted by Pietro de Bonitate and G. B. Mazzolo between the end of the 14C and 1534. It features lions supporting twisted columns and five orders of small statues on either side. In the ogival arch is a *Madonna enthroned with Child* sculpted by G. B. Mazzolo in 1534. In the upper cusp, sculpted by Pietro de Bonitate in 1461-77, is *Christ crowning the Virgin*, with angels in exultation on the three points.

Right: Messina. The Duomo (12C).

THE CLOCK BELL TOWER

The elegant bell tower, 60 m high, stands to the left of the Duomo. Designed by Francesco Valenti, it was inaugurated on 13 August 1933. The mechanical clock, with automatic figures and dials with a perpetual calendar and the phases of the moon, was built by Ungerer, a Strasbourg-based firm, and is considered to be the biggest in the world. On the south side, facing the Duomo, are the dials with the calendar and the solar system. On the west side are automatic sculpted figures referring to religious and historical events of the city's life. Every day, at noon, all the figures on the west side start to move, acting out the spectacle designed by their maker.

Top: Messina. The Duomo. Detail of the bell tower: the calendar dial, 3.5 m in diameter, with an inscription indicating the date of construction of the clock.

Messina. The charming Alcantara Gorge, which attracts crowds of tourists almost all the year round.

GOLE DELL'ALCANTARA

The Alcantara Gorge was formed by the lava erupted in ancient times by the Moio crater, and carved out by the waters of the Alcantara River which reaches the coast on the site where Naxos, the first Greek colony of Sicily, was founded. A visit to the picturesque green scenery, washed by the blue waters of the river, is a must. The river-bed can be reached on foot or by means of a lift which takes visitors down to the entrance of the deep gorge, hemmed in for more than twenty metres between two high lava walls which the natural elements have decorated with fantastic engravings and bizarre cavities, producing a highly scenic effect. The present name of the gorge, formerly called *Onobala*, derives from the Arabic *Al Cantara* (the Bridge), referring to the bridge across the river on the Roman consular road which led from Messina to Catania. The Alcantara River is very picturesque throughout its course, with short rapids alternating with calm, crystalline small lakes and, along the banks, a lush vegetation of rhododendrons, oleanders and tenacious brooms amid bright green crops.

TAORMINA

Tauromenion, the present-day Taormina, was founded by a group of survivors from Naxos, which had been destroyed by Dionysius the Elder, a tyrant of Syracuse, in 404 BC. Andromachus, the father of the historian Timaeus, transferred the survivors to the slopes of Mount Tauro and founded the city in 358 BC. The foundation of the new Greek colony in the eastern part of the island caused the Sicel populations, who had already been forced by the arrival of the first colonists to leave the coast and settle on the nearby Peloritani Mountains, to move further inland. *Tauromenion*, which was never completely independent, was often destroyed by the Greeks and Carthaginians. At the beginning of the First Punic War it sided with the Romans, who occupied it after the death of Hieron II, making it a *civitas foederata*. During the Roman age it witnessed important historical events, such as the slaves' revolt of 132 BC. It was pillaged by Verres, and turned into a colony by Octavian in 34 BC. In Byzantine times it was one of the main strongholds against the Arab conquest of the island. In 902 AD a large part of its population was killed by the Arabs led by the cruel Ibrahim who, before the very eyes of the few survivors, pulled the heart of Bishop Procopius out of his chest and ate it.

Tauromenion enjoyed a short period of peace when the Christians rebuilt it in 913. In 962 the town, again under Arab rule, was named Almoezia from the name of the conqueror, Al-Muizz. In 1079 Roger of Hauteville conquered it after a five-month siege. Rebuilt and embellished with new monuments, the town became an important economic and commercial centre. In 1410 Palazzo Corvaja became the seat of the Sicilian Parliament which met in Taormina to elect Frederick, count de Luna, as king of Sicily. In 1675, during the Messina uprising, the town remained loyal to Spain and was occupied by the French troops of Louis XIV. In the 18C, having lost its former commercial role since the newly-built Messina-Catania road axis excluded the passage of goods and travellers from its area, Taormina became an elite tourist resort thanks to enthusiastic foreign visitors who spread word about its fascinating history and landscape abroad. The town expanded beyond its ancient boundary walls, starting a process of tourist development which has made it one of the most renowned tourist resorts in the world.

Taormina. The "Badia Vecchia" (Old Abbey), or "Badiazza", a Norman building restored in the 14C with decorative motifs of the time. In the background, the smoking summit of Mount Etna.

DUOMO OF SAN NICOLO'

The exterior of the church is simple in style. The façade features a portal decorated with reliefs framed by fine fluted columns in the piers and architrave, and a small 16C eight-mullioned rose window with a cross tracery in the middle. On the left side is a late-15C portal with exquisite floral decorations in the piers and ogival arch. In the centre of the architrave is the figure of Christ blessing,

Above: Taormina. A suggestive view of the town and its breathtaking surroundings.

Right: Taormina.
A night view of the Duomo of San Nicolò, standing in the middle of a square flanked by the road axis where the remains of older buildings and 15C architectural vestiges are to be found.

flanked by St Peter and St Paul. On the right side there is a third portal dating from the mid-16C, with an ogival lunette and an architrave. The interior is divided by six columns into a nave and two aisles. The sacristy houses a rich collection of sacred gold items, dating from various ages. Above the altars are paintings by *Antonino Giuffrè* (1463), a polyptych by *Antonello de Saliba* (1504); an alabaster statue of the Virgin and Child (Gagini school, early 16C), and other exquisite paintings and sculptures.

THE GRAECO-ROMAN THEATRE

The second most important and largest theatre in Sicily, surpassed only by the Greek theatre in Syracuse, it was begun by Greek colonists in the 3C BC, during the tyranny of Hieron II. In Roman Imperial times the building was altered and enlarged. The boundary walls were raised and the cavea widened, while the orchestra was left unchanged. The present aspect probably dates from the 2C AD, when it was almost completely reconstructed by the Romans, who used it for gladiatorial fights. It has a maximum diameter of 109 m (35 m in the orchestra) and could seat up to 5,400 people. The cavea, which exploits the morphology of the land, was divided into nine wedges, with masonry entrance steps. At the top was an external portico with large pillars, part of which has been restored and can still be seen today. The back walls of the stage are still extant, with niches and columns raised during restoration work carried out in 1860. The front had two orders of columns and the stage was flanked by the *parascenia*, rooms used by the actors and to store scenic fittings. In Roman times the theatre was only used for gladiatorial and *venationes* shows. The orchestra was turned into an arena surrounded by a high podium which served to protect the spectators during the performances, and by a service ambulatory with a vault supporting the lower tiers of seats. In

Taormina. The Graeco-Roman Theatre, begun by Greek colonists in the 3C BC, was almost completely reconstructed by the Romans in the 2C AD. From the Theatre there is a magnificent view of the surroundings, with the splendid Ionian coast and Mount Etna in the background.

the centre of the orchestra-arena were some large basins. The theatre still has excellent acoustics. From the top of the steps there is a magnificent view sweeping from the peak of Mount Etna, covered with snow for most of the wintertime, to the peninsula of Schisò, the site of ancient Naxos (the first Greek colony on the island), which seems to stretch out into the blue and peaceful waters of the Ionian Sea.

PALAZZO CORVAJA

This is one of the most elegant aristocratic palaces of the Sicilian 14C-15C, of which two other examples exist at Taormina: the so-called Badia Vecchia (Old Abbey) or *Badiazza*, and the Palazzetto del Duca di Santo Stefano. The palace is a typical 14C square building with merlons and an internal courtyard where a staircase leads up to the piano nobile. The exquisite two- and three-light windows are characterized by small, slender columns. The ogives are surrounded by elegant and sinuous frames. The external façades of the building were, however, left incomplete. The palace was formerly surrounded by a magnificent garden and belonged to several aristocratic families over the centuries. From 10 to 18 August 1411 it was the seat of the Sicilian Parliament summoned by Queen Bianca. As the town began to expand beyond its boundary walls, new buildings were constructed near the palace. Restored in 1946, it became the seat of municipal offices.

Taormina. Isola Bella, once a hermitage.

TAORMINA'S COASTLINE

The coast stretching from the long sandy shore of Letojanni to Capo Taormina is characterized by a succession of rocky promontories, charming bays, small golden beaches, marine caves and "faraglioni" (rock stacks) rising from the sea. On the mythical Ionian Sea, a beautiful natural scenery unfolds: the *Baia delle Sirene* (Sirens' Bay), the cliffs of Capo Sant'Andrea dropping sheer into the sea, the picturesque gulf of *Isola Bella*, the rocky spur of Capo Taormina with the jagged *faraglioni* and the luminous *Grotta Azzurra* (Blue Cave). On the surrounding hills, covered with a lush vegetation and evergreen gardens, are the refined hotel facilities which have made Taormina famous all over the world. The climate is also mild in winter and North-European tourists may happen to be found bathing in the *tepid waters of Mazzarò* in January, when Mount Etna is covered with snow and the early blossom of almond-trees embellishes the gardens. The 18C and 19C travellers who first depicted the charms of Taormina in their paintings or early daguerrotypes were the forerunners of an elite tourist influx of European aristocrats and men of culture from all over the world. Since then, Taormina has developed its tourist industry to become the main tourist resort in Sicily.

Taormina. The picturesque cove of Lido Mazzarò, with the renowned bathing facilities and hotels which create a refined and exclusive atmosphere.

Above: The remains of Naxos, the first Greek colony in Sicily (734 BC).

Right: Milazzo. The photo illustrates the various stages of its urban development. The upper citadel surrounded by the 16C walls, the Borgo with the "Spanish quarters" and the low-lying modern town developing around the port.

NAXOS

Founded in 734 BC by the Chalcidians from Euboea and by the oecist Thucles, Naxos was the first Greek colony in Sicily. Archaeological research has shown traces of earlier settlements dating from the Neolithic Age (Stentinello culture) and the Bronze Age (Thapsos culture). As early as the archaic age, the city became culturally important as the seat of an altar dedicated to *Apollo Archegetes* (Founder), the protector of the Greek colonists in Sicily, built immediately after it was founded. Naxos founded *Leontinoi* (present-day Lentini) in 729 BC, and *Katane* (present-day Catania) in 728 BC. Not far from the city, on a site not yet identified by archaeological research, the inhabitants of Naxos probably founded the city of *Callipolis*. In 495 BC Hippocrates of Gela occupied and partly destroyed the city to oppose the expansionist policy of the Chalcidians. After recovering from this first Doric invasion, Naxos fell under the dominion of the Syracusan Hieron, the brother and successor of Gelon, who deported its population to Leontinoi. In 425 BC it sided with Athens against Syracuse and, after the defeat of Athens in 414 BC, it felt the full sting of the revenge of Dionysius the Elder in 403 BC, when it vanished from history.

Above: Milazzo. The narrow, intensively cultivated peninsula ending at Capo Milazzo, fringed with picturesque coves and brief stretches of sand.

MILAZZO

Evidence of an early Neolithic settlement dating from c 4000 BC has been found in the territory of Milazzo. Between the 9C and 8C BC the site was inhabited by the Sicels, until the foundation of the Greek city of *Mylai* in 649 BC on the lower slopes of the narrow rocky peninsula which characterizes this stretch of coast. Excavations carried out on the site of the necropolis have brought to light a proto-Villanovan cremation burial system from the 10C-8C BC, with bowl-covered urns surrounded by stones. Tomb furnishings from the period following the foundation of the Greek city (8C-7C BC) have also been found in the necropolis, including proto-Corinthian, Ionic and Cycladian pottery. During the Punic Wars, in 260 BC, the battle between Carthaginians and Romans, won by Consul Caius Duilius, was fought in the waters off Milazzo. In medieval times the city was fortified, and in the 13C Frederick II Hohenstaufen built a castle which incorporated a 12C tower situated at the top of the promontory overlooking the town. Later, in the mid-15C, King Alfonso "the Magnanimous" (of Aragon and Sicily) built a fortified stretch of walls to defend the east side of the castle. This is the first example in Sicily of walls with bastions, that is fortifications suitable for the use of the newly-introduced firearms and of canons against siege batteries. The top of the promontory thus became a true citadel, where public offices and the houses of the administrative class also stood. Between the 16C and 17C massive walls with bastions were built on the east edge of the promontory, in accordance with the latest contrivances of the military architecture of the time: large angular bulwarks, casemates, ravelins, etc. This is the greatest Renaissance defensive system in Sicily, designed by a group of talented military architects of the time. A new cathedral was also built within these boundary walls. An interesting excursion can be made to the Capo Milazzo lighthouse, with its splendid view of the Aeolian islands, the Calabrian coast and the Nebrodi and Peloritani mountains. A flight of steps near the lighthouse leads up to the rock sanctuary where St Anthony of Padua, travelling from Africa to Lisbon, took refuge during a storm.

Above: Lipari. View of the town, the main centre of the Aeolian islands, with the medieval stronghold.

Bottom: Lipari. Punta della Crapazza, on the southern coast.

Opposite page, top: The magnificent panorama from the edge of the Gran Cratere della Fossa on the island of Vulcano.

Opposite page, bottom: Vulcano.

AEOLIAN OR LIPARI ISLANDS

The Aeolian islands, the "seven sisters", are of Quaternary volcanic origin and were formed as a result of the millenary accumulation of erupted material and consequent raising of the sea floor. Only two volcanoes of the vast original system are still active today. *Vulcano*, which last erupted in 1888-90, now limits its activity to the emission of hot sulphurous gases. *Stromboli* still has a cyclic eruptive activity, accompanied by explosions of scoriae, lava and vapours which are thrown high into the sky before rushing headlong into the sea following pathways known as "sciare di fuoco", torrents of fire. Archaeological research has continued uninterrupted since 1946 thanks to the Soprintendenza ai Beni Culturali (Cultural Heritage Authority) of Eastern Sicily. The discovery of decorated pottery in the style peculiar to the so-called Stentinello culture on the rocky spurs of Lipari has suggested that the settlements on the island, from the 4th millennium BC onwards, were the result of migratory flows from the Sicilian coasts. After various periods classified as Milazzese, Ausonius I and II (from 1400 BC to

the 7C BC), Greek civilization began in 580 BC, when the Cnidians, back from the unsuccessful expedition led by Pentathlus, landed at Lipari and founded their colony (Diodorus Siculus). Until the Roman conquest, Lipari followed the changing fortunes of Sicily in the wider context of the secular struggles between Greeks, Carthaginians and Romans to gain control of the island. In 836 AD the Arabs destroyed Lipari, and it was only under the Great Count of Sicily Roger I, in 1083, that the island and the archipelago rose from their ruins, also thanks to an active group of Benedictine monks who founded a monastery on the ancient Acropolis with royal permission.

Above: Tindari. The Sanctuary of the "Madonna di Tindari" with a view of the small Vergolo, Verde and Marinello lagoons, enclosed by pebble banks continually altered in contour and width by the action of the sea.

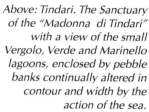

Bottom: Tindari. The remaining columns of a Roman house dating from the 1C AD.

TINDARI

Founded in 396 BC by Dionysius the Elder, it was one of the latest Greek colonies in Sicily. It stands on a stretch of level ground on the top of the Capo Tindari promontory, on a picturesque site overlooking the sea. The Greek *Tyndaris* was a prosperous centre and witnessed a monumental urban development, particularly in Roman times. A loyal Roman ally during the Punic Wars, it was a privileged city during the Imperial age. It was built to a regular plan, with wide parallel streets (*decumani*) crossed by a series of perpendicular narrow lanes (*cardines*) forming the *insulae*, blocks of private houses with rooms arranged around a peristyle, flanked by shops and *tabernae*. In the early centuries of Christianity and under the Byzantines it was raised to a diocese, but it was completely destroyed during the Arab conquest. On the highest point of

Capo Tindari is the sanctuary housing the Byzantine wooden statue of the *Black Madonna*, highly venerated and traditionally believed to be of Oriental origin. The sanctuary was built in 1549 on the site of a pre-existing one, after the town was devastated and sacked by the North-African pirate Ariadeno Barbarossa.

Above: Tindari. The so-called "Basilica" or "Gymnasium", perhaps the seat of public assemblies in the 4C AD.

A SHORT DIGRESSION: SICILIAN COOKING

Taken from
"Sicilian Cooking"
by Carmelo Sammarco
© Arnone Editore - Palermo

Translation:
Quid Traduzioni e Servizi Linguistici (P. Duckworth)

Photographs: Carmelo Sammarco
Drawing: Rodo Santoro

Much has been written about Sicilian cooking. Doubts have been raised about the origin of sauces and dishes which reflect the nature and the inheritance of the various peoples who have inhabited the island. Without doubt, this has some truth to it. However, it is more realistic to consider Sicily's central position in the Mediterranean region. From the times of pre-history, this sea has united rather than divided its surrounding countries.

It is not easy to characterise Sicily. It is a place of violent passions, agonising melancholy and incredible contrasts. It is a microcosm which presents, in miniature form, all the components of a continent with a sufficiently mild climate, which changes as we move inland from the coast.

It has the most varied colours, enlivened by the sun. This explains all the various hues of blue of the sky and the sea, the various hues of green of the fields and the woods and the various dazzling whites, yellows and reds of the flowers. The crops have always been diversified and, to a certain degree, extended. First, we have a mature fruit near the coast, then in the hills and, finally, in the mountains. For a land where agriculture was the dominating activity, this is particularly important. All kinds of plants take root and prosper without problems.

Surrounded by such bountiful nature, the Sicilian loves colours. Grey skies, lead-coloured seas and flat landscapes oppress and upset him, as if they were physical and moral ills. Colour means joy, it means party-time, it means happiness. As we will see later, the cake, symbol of the party, is a celebration of colours, to feast with the eyes before the palate. It does not matter where these colours come from. What matters is that the table is always very rich. This explains the recent fortune of the kiwi fruit, an Australian fruit which is not especially tasty but is of an intense, brilliant green, animated by white and with small black rays. This is the same green which we find in a less intense form in the imitation fresh fruit, made with marzipan to a recipe which has varied little from ancient times as it has been passed down through the ages. The Romans, in particular, loved the produce of the island, especially Hyblaean honey, and they had a high opinion of the expertise of Sicilian cooks.

Sicilians also owe most of their spices, not to the Arabs, but to antiquity. These spices, together with the aromatic herbs, fill the island and give Sicilian cooking mysterious smells and tastes, with a vaguely Oriental feel. Dill, absinthe, juniper, garlic, onion, cloves, ginger, basil, pepper, cinnamon, cassia, cardamom, cumin, cinnamomum, coriander, fennel, laurel, lentiscus, sweet marjoram, oregano, mint, lavender, nutmeg, rosemary, rocket salad, sage, celery, saffron. All of these spices are listed in the archives of Alexandria of Egypt, a type of fixed price, which dates back to the 4th century AD.

The spices, many of which had medicinal properties, were used to preserve as well as flavour the dishes. They flavoured sauces made with honey and vinegar which dress roasted or boiled vegetables, meat and fish, which date back to Roman times. This is documented by *Apicio*, gourmet and connoisseur of the 1st century AD.

Before the cities had large squalid public lodging areas, the people lived together in the suburbs and in the city centre. The noble palaces, the town houses and humble cottages had open balconies and terraces (*astrachi*), where you found geraniums and begonias amongst the basil and mint. They tried to recreate the country, the green which is always present in the heart of the people. These terraces were like a multicoloured backdrop for the streets and courtyards. The impression was a vast, everchanging stage representing the tragi-comedy of man.

Religious or civil feasts, family occasions: baptisms, weddings, funerals - any event was an excuse to prepare eloquent meals following an age-old menu with precise rituals: no meal worth its name had less than fifteen courses.

To start with, a consommé was more than sufficient to warm up the stomach. This was followed by the first courses (usually a very elaborate pasta). The second courses, meat and fish, were alternated with middle dishes and other delights, such as charcuteries, cheese, crushed olives, pickles, sun-dried tomatoes and whatever else was available!

130

The middle dishes came in all kinds of varieties: omelettes with vegetables, cheese and vegetable pies (aubergines, tomatoes, peppers, courgettes), filled and drowned in spicy or sweet sauces. However, the main middle dish was the so-called "mixed fry". "A meal without a fry is not a meal", according to those in the know.

Croquettes - rice, potato, semolina, milk, cream -, sliced cheeses, brain, spinal marrow, vegetables coated with breadcrumbs or with delicate batters followed one another in waves, hot and crispy, presented on large oblong trays adorned with fresh lettuce leaves.

With the passing of time and new cooking ideas, the abundant middle dishes, reduced in quantity, to make room for side dishes, gradually took on the role of starters and appetisers, not part of traditional Sicilian cuisine.

* * *

Sicilian cuisine has two undoubted sovereigns - when you don't want to consider them as guardian divinities - loved and venerated by everyone on the island: bread and pasta. It may be true that in recent times, their power has been threatened many times and they have been endlessly accused, sent to trial and abolished by supporters of the hard line. "You eat with bread", children used to be advised. Nowadays, pre-packaged snacks are preferred and, although they are guaranteed, they are not very wholesome. Our old sovereign, bread, was praised, sung about and revered during the Fascist period, especially during the time of the sanctions. We can consider bread to be a victim of political persecution that, sent into exile, was replaced by toasted bread, asphyxial breadsticks and *crackers*. A genuine Sicilian knows well that once you have left the Strait, it is better to make as little use of bread as possible. In this way, it takes on the aspect of a nostalgic memory.

Flour, water, and natural yeast. The dough, moulded into rounded or extended shapes (loafs, *pupe* and *picciriddi*) were lovingly wrapped in sheets of wool to help the leavening process and then cooked in earthenware and olive vine sarment ovens, red-hot from the flames. In the country areas, the dough was very compact. Bread was only made, in fact, a couple of times a month and the bread had to be edible for a very long time. Once it hardened, cooked with laurel, garlic and vegetable stock, it became a hot good-smelling soup. Fresh bread from the oven, with oil, oregano, salt, pepper, anchovies and a sprinkling of *pecorino*, was a choice dish.

In the city, bread was processed softer and white. Packed in various forms and enriched with sesame or poppy seeds, it was almost sweet. There was a distinction among strong bread, Spanish bread and French bread. The dough was different and they were eaten with different kinds of meals. Finally, small loafs *(muffulette* and *guastedde)* filled with chopped meat or ricotta and cheese or ricotta cream, candied fruit and chocolate *(iris)* turned the bread into a complete meal.

* * *

Some say it came to Sicily from China after the travels of Marco Polo. Others say that it has always existed on the island. The other sovereign, pasta, after a period of being neglected, if not actually ignored, returned to its rightful place in the kitchen as a result of the discovery of the Mediterranean diet. In truth, the Sicilians, from the coast to the mountains, have always regarded it highly, as a pillar of their cuisine. From its earliest forms, prepared by hand: *tagliolini* (thin noodles), *quadrucci* (square noodles), *anelletti* (rings), *cavateddi* and *busi* (holed shaped pasta), with the arrival of pasta-making machines, a series of shapes has been developed for which there are two main lines: long pasta, to be wrapped around the fork and short pasta. Every pasta shape requires a special type of sauce.

Sumptuously wrapped in sweet or hot crusts or covered with a thin layer of breadcrumbs, with a sauce or in soup, pasta reigns over a nutritious team of handmaids

and pageboys: the sauces. Nowadays, it is difficult to think that they had to do without tomato, as the image of spaghetti is commonly linked to tomato and basil sauce. We must remember that we cannot be sure that we owe the discovery of this vegetable to Christopher Columbus, given that some scholars identify in the tomato the famous fruits of the Hesperides related to the tale of Hercules. In any case, returning to the sauces, they range from the most simple garlic, oil and chilli pepper and its variants (with parsley, anchovies and toasted breadcrumbs) to elaborate sauces including all kinds of vegetables and legumes boiled or browned with aromatic herbs: healthy, tasty seasonings. Other sauces include: cheese *(tozzo)*, ricotta with fried courgettes and aubergines, as well as a number of soups with fish, shellfish, seafood, chopped meat and giblets. To summarise, pasta is the main dish and sometimes the only dish in a meal.

Rice was eaten less frequently. Imported from the East, perhaps from the Arabs, it passed through the island, leaving few but tasty reminders (timbales, rice patties, croquettes, sweet and hot pancakes, creamed rice and sweet rice ice cream) and then moved on to areas which are more suitable for its cultivation.

As for sweet corn, which came from the West Indies, it was considered bran feed for chicken! Every month, there are two or three obligatory religious or civil feasts in Sicily. If we add private parties: birthdays, Saint's days, etc., there is a considerable number of occasions. In any case, both public and private parties were a time for one or more family clans to get together.

Conversations were held in the parlours of the aristocrats (from the cavaliers to the princes, there were quite a few). Arts, trades and professions united the members of the various associations: the brotherhoods and sisterhoods. The less well-to-do socialised daily in the courtyards and the alleys. Dressed in the most elegant of clothes, this colourful representation of humanity, went about the streets adorned in colour and light, showing themselves off in the holiday "parade". After all, dressing up is also an essential part of the Sicilian spirit.

It was essential to interrupt the walks *(u passiu)* with a stop-off in the cafés, a sanctuary for one's thirst, bedecked with all kinds of cakes and desserts, in every shape and colour. The dessert was such a part of the celebration ritual that it ended up characterising it: for example, the *buccellato* (ring-shaped cake) represents Christmas; the *sfincie* (cream puffs) represent Saint Joseph's Day, the *cassata* represents Easter, the *cannolo* represents Carnival and marzipan fruit represents All Souls' Day. We must also consider that some ingredients, apart from jams and preserves, were only available in certain periods of the year. For example, ricotta (November to April), watermelon (June to August), citrus fruits (November to April), just to mention a few.

Sicilian pastries, as we have already said, are mostly very rich. They are very sweet, extremely colourful and a joy to be beheld. The colours, when they cannot be created with raw materials, are created with multicoloured icing sugar and chocolate. This is topped with candied fruit or marzipan fruits, or aniseed wrapped with coloured sugar, or cylinders and balls of sweetened flour in a variety of colours: yellow, green, blue, red *(mbriaculicchi* and *cannettiglie)* and silver and golden balls and tablets.

No small or large centre in Sicily worth its name is without one or more typical cakes or desserts. It is impossible to remember all of them. Here are a few examples: the *"aranciata"* from Modica; the *pignoccata* from Messina; the *"testa di turco"* (fried pastry with cream) from Castelbuono, cheese cakes from Polizzi, the *"ossa di morto"* from Sciacca and the *cassata* from Palermo, the latter needing absolutely no description at all. Common to the whole island, we have *pasticciotti* made from almond-flour, short pastry and sweetened bread paste, filled with jams, preserves and custard. Among these, we have the famous *"minni di virgini"* (virgins' breasts) in eternal memory of Saint Agatha, patron saint of Catania and co-patron saint of Palermo.

Even the most concise of summaries of Sicilian cakes and sweets must include at least a brief description of the methods for preserving fruit, cooking it with sugar or in spirit or julep. The latter produced tasty syrups to be served cold and diluted as thirst-quenching drinks in the summer heat as an alternative to fresh squeezed juices.

Mixed with fish glue, the fruit juices had the consistency of soft gelatine (coffee, mulberry, wild black cherry) or were consolidated with starch as in the melon gel, a typical product of Palermo, with a faint odour of jasmine.

Fruit juices, essences, even spices are essential ingredients in the preparation of crushed ice drinks *(granite)*, sorbets *(sorbetti)* and ice cream, other undoubted masterpieces of our cuisine. In the past, when artificial ice had not yet been discovered, the winter snow was preserved in holes and cracks covered with straw and rags. Long rows of mules came down from the mountains, bringing the residual snow used to cool the liquids until they were solid. According to the solidity and the creaminess of the compound, there was a distinction among soft ice creams *(cremolate)*, crushed ice drinks *(granite)*, sorbets *(sorbetti)* and ice creams. Ice cream was enriched with candied fruit, hazelnuts and chopped almonds. As well as the fruit juices, ice cream was flavoured with coffee, chocolate, cinnamon *(scorzonera)*, jasmine and mint.

***

Bacchus, the god of wine, bringing grapes from the Indies, gave wine to the mortals, a real panacea which brought joy. At least, this is what the Greeks who, it is said, then introduced wine to Sicily believed. It is surely no coincidence that the most ancient Sicilian colony, Naxos, used the Silenus as money. This was a figure of the Dionysian court holding the Kantharos, the typical drinking vessel. We now know that wild grapevine was common in a large part of the temperate area which includes most of the Mediterranean basin and that Greek mythology is attributed something which, after all, is a common legacy.

The strong and dense Sicilian wine, appreciated from ancient times, has long been used in Italy and abroad to prepare weaker wines. Only recently, our wines, treated with expertise, are becoming common in ever-vaster areas and markets.

From the dry whites of the area of Alcamo, to the reds of the Southern tip of the island - the cerasuolo wine of Vittoria and the nero of Pachino - now we have a whole series of quality-approved wines like those from the slopes of Etna. To these, we can add the wines treated with raisins or strongly sweetened wines, typical of the volcano areas of Pantelleria *(passito* wine, *muscatel* wine) and Lipari *(malvasia* wine). Nor do Sicilian wines lack a famous exponent. In fact, in the 18th century, Giovanni Meli, a famous poet from Palermo, sung the praises of the qualities of every single wine and, at the same time, criticised the pretensions of those who, having bottled and labelled it, sold the wine as if it were nectar from France. This was vanity of fashion, snobbish xenomania which is found in the habit of accompanying desserts with dry sparkling wines *(brut* or *extra-brut)* or, after dinner, guzzling whisky or cognac instead of the mistreated sweet wines.

Now, however, there has been a change in habits. It may be the current crisis or a change in taste that has led the people to look at the notebooks of their ancestors, the secrets of the convents, containing recipes for sweet wines and liquors and, with a slight change in the dose of the syrup, liquors made with citrus fruits, verbena, orange-blossom, mint, coffee, the ratafia of mulberries, strawberries, blackberries, walnut, herb and spice compounds mixed in various ways known as *centerbe* or *amari* (bitter aperitifs) and, finally, the age-old *anisetta* (aniseed cordial).

Elda Joly

CONTENTS

Printed by: Officine Grafiche Riunite - Palermo
March 2004